Library of Congress Cataloging-in-Publication Data

Silber, Earle, The Baker's Son: Tales of My Baltimore Childhood

Summary: A retired psychoanalyst shares his memories of growing up in a Jewish family in Depression-era Baltimore

ISBN: 978-1-939282-03-3

Published by Miniver Press, LLC, McLean Virginia
Copyright 2013 Miniver Press

First edition February 2013

THE BAKER'S SON: TALES OF MY BALTIMORE CHILDHOOD

EARLE SILBER

2013

North Monroe Street

Baltimore

1931

`

To my wife, Judith, who was my first audience for these tales of my childhood. As I finished writing each chapter I could hardly wait to show it to her to read. Her questions and comments were insightful and helpful. Talking with her about what I had written enabled us to learn more about each other, even after more than twenty-five years of marriage. Her appreciation of my writing and her encouragement made this book possible. For that I am profoundly grateful.

INTRODUCTION

In 1925, I was born in Baltimore into the Silber family and given the name *Yisruel,* a Hebrew name that was miraculously transformed into "Earle" in English. I had four older brothers, Bernard, Sam, Sidney, and Myer; two older sisters, Rosalie and Libbye; and a younger sister, Evelyn, who was born five years after I was. My father founded Silber's Bakery, as renowned for its rye bread as it was for its famous chocolate drop cookies.

We lived on a main thoroughfare in northwest Baltimore and occupied two row houses, 1725 and 1727 North Monroe Street. These houses were remodeled into a bakery and sales store; we lived in the remaining rooms on the first floor and the second floor above the bakery.

We grew up in an all-white neighborhood of predominantly working and lower middle class families. Baltimore was thoroughly segregated: separate neighborhoods, schools, hospital entrances and wards, bathrooms, drinking fountains and movie theatres. Neighborhoods were separated not only by race, but also by religion. McKean Avenue, east of my street, Monroe Street, divided Catholic families from our neighborhood where Jewish families of eastern European origin lived. German Jewish families lived in yet another part of Baltimore.

Silber's Bakery was a successful, bustling business. As a result, we never wanted for necessities at a time when many of our neighbors were still bearing the brunt of the Depression. People lined up at the side door of the bakery for leftover bread during those hard times. We listened to the radio and took in every word of FDR's fireside chats. We had a milkman who delivered milk to our door as well as someone who regularly supplied us with ice. There were no refrigerators, but "ice boxes," which required almost daily replenishing, especially during the broiling, hot Baltimore summer months.

My grandmother, aunts, uncles, and cousins lived within a radius of four or five blocks from our home. We could walk to grocery stores, public transportation, drugstores, dry goods stores, Easterwood Park, elementary school, a branch of the Enoch Pratt Library, a bank, our synagogue, and three local movie theatres, the *Fulton*, *Metropolitan* and *Schanze*.

I attended a public elementary school, P.S. 29, and my classmates became my closest friends. There was a nearby empty lot that became our playing field for pick-up games of softball. We had penknives that were used only for playing a very safe game called numbly-peg. There were occasional fistfights but I never remember anyone being killed in our neighborhood and, as far as I knew, no one had guns.

`

When I was twelve, I traveled by streetcar, one block from our home, to attend a special Junior High School, P.S. 49, in downtown Baltimore. I completed high school at Baltimore City College, a public, all-boys school, when I was sixteen.

So, how did I happen to write this book about memories of my childhood? It was written by accident. It was not planned. I had no intention of writing a book, but only a single story about my father. Here's how it all began:

Some years ago, in a conversation with a friend who had just attended a funeral, I was reminded of my father's funeral and how painful it had been for me. My friend asked if I had ever thought about writing about this. I hadn't. But, after giving it some thought, I decided it might not be a bad idea. So I wrote what I remembered about my father and about his funeral. When I finished writing, I felt a great sense of relief.

`

Weeks later, I remembered what it was like to go grocery shopping with my mother when I was a child. I was surprised at how vivid that memory was and my recall of many of the details of that experience. I wrote about that next. Then, some time later, other memories bubbled to the surface. I continued to write about them in no particular sequence, but simply as each memory emerged. The more I wrote, the more I remembered. I wrote this collection over a period of five or six years, with long intervals in between writing each episode.

At some point, I began to realize that I was living out a task of old age: putting my life history in some order by reminiscing. Years ago, my colleague and friend, Robert Butler, a psychoanalyst interested in ageing, had described this period of life as a time for "life review," a time to put the past in perspective. He viewed reminiscing in a positive way, as coming to terms with

`

one's life history as the end of life approaches. I had entered into this work without realizing it. So, writing this book was not entirely an accident after all.

Growing old need not mean an end to psychological development. Just as each phase of life, beginning in infancy, brings with it certain tasks, so does the last part of life. Having the good luck to recently celebrate my eighty-eighth birthday, I have had time to reminisce and to write about my childhood.

Although I am now retired as a psychoanalyst, my interest in observing and understanding the complexity of memory has not diminished. Trying to notice what events in my present life evoke these old memories continues to intrigue me. Not always, but sometimes, I was able to recognize the connection of the past with a current event in my life. For example, some time after writing the story I called *One of the Last to Go*—a memory of

`

being among the last to leave summer camp as friend after friend said goodbye— I realized that I had recalled this at a very significant time in my recent life. Several of my friends had died within a short period of time. Once again, I was saying goodbye and was among the last to go. I was experiencing the same sadness in the present that I did many years ago when, one by one, my friends left camp before I did.

I found the process of remembering and writing to have a very "settling" effect on me. Writing was different than talking about memories, as I had done during many hours of treatment, with various psychoanalysts. Writing provided me with an acceptance of my past, in all of its complexities. As I wrote, I also became aware of new insights about my relationship with each of my parents.

As a matter of style, I decided to fashion my memories into *stories;* that is, without

`

altering facts, to find coherent themes; organize, not meander and to make my recollections into interesting writing. Whether these accounts are what "really" happened, I will never be certain.

Sharing my stories with my siblings had the unintended consequence of opening up more conversations about our early lives. There were expected differences in our memories about unimportant details—the name of our neighborhood movie theatre, for example. On the other hand, there were significant differences in our memories of each other and of our parents. But, of more importance, I appreciated in a more significant way, that each of us grew up in a different family. What I have written are *my* memories of growing up in *my* family.

There was one more thing that motivated me to continue writing: my ignorance of my parents' early lives. My mother and father never talked about their childhoods. I did not want my children or

`

grandchildren to be left with the same
void. I wanted them to know more about
who I was, without editing out the painful
or embellishing the happy parts. To do so
would have meant erasing a part of myself.

March 2013
E.S.

CONTENTS

1

HALAVAH

The best times were when my mother would take me shopping on Saturday night. She never asked me to go. She announced that she was going to the grocery store and I was coming with her. That was better than an invitation. She wanted me to go.

Although I accompanied her many times, in what must have been every season, I only remember the nights being warm when we left the house together. We walked down the sidewalk on Monroe Street, and past Miss Brinkley's house next door. Miss Brinkley was very kind and sweet, a frail woman, bent with age. Sometimes during the day, I would ring Miss Brinkley's doorbell, wait for her to appear, and then present a small pot and ask if we could have some dirt. (Our back yard had been sacrificed to create an oven on the back of

18

the bakery, so we had no source of soil with which to grow plants indoors). She would oblige by going to her garden and bringing back my reward: my pot now overflowing with rich dirt, and ready for planting.

Onward, we passed the Friedmans, and said hello to them and the other neighbors who might be sitting on their porch or on their front steps. Then, we came to an alley near the end of the block. I always crossed it quickly. In one of the garages, there were butchers who killed chickens. But these men were no ordinary butchers. They killed the chickens in a special way to make them kosher. They were called *schochets*.

I was afraid to go down that alley, afraid to witness the work of the schochets. But of course, at some point, I went down there and saw it for myself.

`

There were many crates filled with chickens, all squeezed together and making lots of noise. They were trying to get out. I watched with horror at what happened next. The schochet reached into a crate and grabbed one of the chickens by its legs. This is the part I didn't like to watch but I couldn't stop looking. The chicken flapped its wings frantically and helplessly. The schochet lifted the chicken by its legs so its head was upside down. He had a knife. He slit the chicken's throat and cut off its head. Blood started coming out. Then the schochet swung the chicken around and around to get more blood out. Then he hung the chicken upside down so all the blood would finish coming out. He stuffed the chicken's raw, bleeding neck into a funnel to make sure its body had no blood left in it. That was how you made a chicken kosher. I walked away very fast. I tried not to remember what I saw. But I could never forget.

I walked quickly to the corner house. That was a much better place. Mrs. Wrench, who lived there, "took in laundry." She washed curtains for people who lived in our neighborhood. There was no garage but an open space, filled with large wooden frames on which lace curtains were stretched to be dried. She also ran a small "snowball" stand. We placed our orders. She leaned into a block of ice with a small aluminum shaver, scraping icy mounds of snow which she scooped out into small cardboard trays (the three-cent size) or large plastic cups (the five-cent size). Then the snowballs were drenched with sweet syrups. If you ordered the five-cent cup, you could even get some marshmallow on the top for free. She had every flavor in the world you could think of. The ones I remember are strawberry, cherry, grape, orange, and even chocolate, my favorite. Her snowballs were the standard by which I judged all others in my lifetime. None has ever surpassed them.

Shearer's grocery store was across the street, on the corner at the end of the block. We waited for a break in the traffic (Monroe Street was also Route One, a main thoroughfare through Baltimore) and crossed over to the store. We entered on the Monroe Street side into a vast array of shelves stacked with canned goods, boxes of cereal, pasta; display cases full of cheeses, milk, sour cream; crates of vegetables and fruit. Mrs. Shearer was behind the counter, wearing an apron stained with pickle juice and a variety of sauces. My mother had no list, but looked around and asked for whatever caught her eye. Sometimes she wanted a box of Wheaties on the top shelf. Mrs. Shearer was an expert at manipulating a long, funny pole with grab bars at the end. She arranged the pole in front of the box, the arms of the pole open to seize their target. Then, as she deftly squeezed the handle, the arms grasped the box and she pulled it off the shelf. The box of Wheaties fell into

Mrs. Shearer's hands and she deposited it on the counter. What a great performance!

Pickles floated in a barrel of brine. My mother indicated which pickle in particular she wanted. Mrs. Shearer pushed up her sleeves, thrust her hand into the barrel, pulled out the designated pickle, wrapped it in heavy paper and then wiped her hands on her apron. My mother proceeded around the store, pointing to whatever she needed. Cheese was not packaged, but stored in blocks in the refrigerated case. Mrs. Sharer cut off huge hunks. Sour cream was ladled into a small container. Everything was placed together on the counter. When all was gathered, Mrs. Shearer tore off a piece of wrapping paper from the large roll on the counter.

She took a pencil from behind her ear, brought the tip of the pencil to her mouth to moisten it and then began the task of adding up my mother's purchases. As she put each item into a large bag, she wrote down its cost. The list of numbers grew. When all had been accounted for, she began the laborious task of adding the figures. I listened with great admiration as she counted aloud, four and eight is twelve and seven is nineteen...carry the ten and four is fourteen.... Every once in a while, the pencil had to be moistened and brought to her mouth for more saliva. Finally she announced the total and my mother counted out the money from a small clasped purse she carried with her. The shopping was complete. But only in *that* part of the store.

We went through a door at the back of the store and entered a small anteroom. To the right was a stairway that led to rooms where the Shearers lived above the store. Straight ahead was another door. We opened it to the butcher shop where Mr. Shearer presided. The smell was quite different. It was a cooler smell. It was a mixture of raw flesh, fat, and blood—a sharp, but not offensive smell. Large slabs of meat hung from hooks inside cases cooled with large blocks of ice.

A large butcher block was the stage upon which Mr. Shearer performed carving magic. He began by unhooking a large slab of meat and slapping it onto the block. Then he sharpened a large, heavy knife, honing it first on one side and then the other of a long, tapered metal sharpener. Mr. Shearer's hands trembled as his knife approached its prey. I was transfixed. How could he possibly cut into the meat with such shaky hands? But—since this was magic—as he reached his target, his hands instantly became steady and his movements were controlled and purposeful. He skillfully sliced off the desired piece of meat, and tossed it up on the scale. It weighed no more nor less than the exact amount my mother had asked for.

We left the butcher shop and went back through the doorway into the grocery store. There my mother made one more

`

purchase. Sometimes I would be afraid she would forget. But she never did. The *halavah*!

There were three blocks of halavah on the counter: one chocolate, one plain, and another marbled with meandering chocolate rivulets. She asked me which kind I would like. It was always hard to decide, but I usually chose the kind that had chocolate mixed in. Mrs. Shearer cut off a piece of halavah, wrapped it in waxed paper and gave it to me. Halavah is beyond sweet. It defines sweetness. It crumbles in the mouth and becomes a sticky, flaky, satisfying, chewy, rich candy. But its taste and texture had yet another secret ingredient: the delicious exhilaration of having a little bit of time alone with my mother.

I ate the halavah bit by bit on the way home, savoring each bite as we trundled back up Monroe Street with our packages. I never thought for a moment that I would

`

save any of the halavah for my brothers
and sisters. I wanted it all to myself.

2

A SAFE HAVEN

I pulled the sheet over my eyes. It didn't stop the flashes of light. Then there was a crashing sound. The sky was angry. I tried to snuggle deeper into the bed. But it wouldn't stop. The light kept flashing and the noise got louder. It sounded like a tree cracking in half. I was really scared. Then I heard the rain. Every time the loud noise came, the window in my room would rattle. I didn't know what to do.

I couldn't think. I was getting more and more scared. My body decided for me. I sat up. I slipped out from under the covers, swung my feet over the edge of the bed and stood still. I was frozen. The bright light came again and this time the big noise came very fast and was ten times louder. My feet began to move.

`

With quick, careful steps I went out of my room. I didn't know where my feet were taking me. I turned left and moved down the hall. I went past the stairway and headed straight for my parents' bedroom. I pushed on the door. No noise. I was even more afraid I might wake my father. That would be worse than the light and the loud noises. Now I remembered the word for what was happening. It was called a storm. My father had storms and they were much worse. I didn't want to wake him up. So I got up on my tiptoes as I turned and moved toward the end of his bed.

I went past the big cabinet that stood against the wall in my parents' room. It was called a chiffarobe and it held most of their clothes. Then I turned right along the foot of my father's bed. On my left was the table where my mother fixed up her face. It was like a desk only it had three tall mirrors on top and a little bench in front of it. There were bottles on the table and something with a little hose and a ball my mother squeezed to make perfume spray out.

Then I passed a chest with drawers where there were more clothes. I could still see the bright flashes of light that came through the windows. At last, I was standing at the side of my mother's bed. I was tall enough to see over the top of her bed. She was sound asleep. I didn't move. I didn't say anything. I just stood there. I waited.

Finally my mother began to stir. After a long, long time, she slowly turned in her bed. I could see her face and I started to feel better. I was quiet. So was my mother. Then she lifted her arm and held up the blanket that was covering her. Even though she didn't say so, I knew she wanted me to climb in under the sheets with her. So I did. It was like being in a cave. It was dark inside the cave, but not scary.

Nothing was scary anymore. I was in a warm, quiet place. Nothing could hurt me. The flashes of light didn't bother me. I could hardly hear the loud sounds anymore. I knew everything would be all right. It felt good to snuggle against my mother's body. I began to doze off. I was not scared. I fell asleep. I was safe at last.

`

3

TWO WEEKS

One day my mother disappeared. I was six. I woke one morning and went from my room into my parents' bedroom. My mother was not there. I walked downstairs, through the living room and into the kitchen. Not there. There was a door from the kitchen that led into the bakery. I opened it, went down the steps into the bakery and looked into the store. Not there, either. No one seemed to care. Maybe she was hiding. My mother was huge. She always wore a big white apron when she worked in the store. It would be

`

hard for her to hide. Why wasn't anybody worried about my mother? Where had she gone?

Mary and Mozella, the black women who took care of me, were already in the house working in the back room on the second floor where they did the laundry. They would certainly tell me where my mother was. I went back into the kitchen, living room, up the stairs, crossed the hall, down past the bedrooms to the back room. Where's Mommy? They looked blank, gave a weak smile and looked down. Something must be terribly wrong. Where's Mommy? They would not say.

The next strange thing that happened was that my aunt Katie was in the house, but she wasn't just visiting. She was upstairs. She was putting away clothes in my parents' room. She was standing in front of the big chifforobe arranging my mother's dresses. Where's Mommy? She shrugged her shoulders. She said something, but her

`

words did not make any sense to me. I understood that she did not want to talk about it and did not want me to ask. No one talked about it.

I do not really remember the next day or the next or the next. My memory of that period exists only in little fragments. I mainly recall it as a cloud that had descended over my life. I did not know the meaning of death. I only recall that I believed that my mother had gone away, that something terrible must have happened and as one day led to the next, I believed I would never see her again. Aunt Katie's presence was of no comfort to me. It only confirmed my mother's absence. Mary and Mozella came every day. They had always taken care of me, washed me, fed me, and looked after me. They must have comforted me.

My father got up early each morning to work in the bakery. I saw little of him during the day and, like everyone else, he

`

said nothing about my mother's disappearance. I must have gone into their bedroom every morning, still searching for my lost mother. I hoped I would wake up one day and find her home again. What happened next, I remember clearly.

It was a bright, sunny day in May, I was in my parents' bedroom, this time peering out the windows that overlooked Monroe Street. I was constantly searching for my mother. Cars streamed up and down the street. As if in slow motion, one of the cars stopped in front of the bakery. The car had writing on it, so it was a taxi. The door of the taxi opened and my father got out. Why wasn't he working in the bakery? Where had he gone? Why was he in a taxi? What I saw next is infused with bright sunlight. My mother was back.

I watched transfixed with disbelief. She bent over to clear the doorway of the taxi and stepped carefully onto the running board and then onto the sidewalk. She was

`

carrying something cradled in her arms. She must have been shopping. There were lots of blankets. In the next instant, I ran out of the bedroom into the hall, flew down the stairs, streaked through the living room, flung open the front door, dashed across the porch, soared down the stairs, and raced across the sidewalk to my mother. I tried to hug her but she wouldn't let go of the bundle, so I wrapped myself around her legs to hold onto her, making sure she would never go away again.

What was wrapped up in all the blankets? My mother lifted one of the covers, so I could get a better look. It was a baby. I had never seen such a tiny baby. It was a girl. My mother took her upstairs and opened one of the bureau drawers, which had already been padded with blankets. That must be where the baby was going to sleep. That was how I learned that I had a sister. Her name was Evelyn.

`

The rest is epilogue, filled in by other bits and pieces of the story I learned about when I was older. I do not remember talking with my brothers and sisters about the birth of my sister until much later in my life. We were together as children, exchanging words but never really speaking to one another about what was in the center of our lives. Sometimes I would imagine that I had made up the story about Evelyn. But my sister, Libbye, two years older, told me that when my mother was away she had discovered baby clothes in the drawers of my mother's dresser. She had shown them to Aunt Katie, who, once again, shrugged and told Libbye she had no idea why they were there. She recalled this time in our lives in exactly the way I had. We shared the same memories.

Many years later, I overheard my mother telling Aunt Katie that the only time she had a real vacation was after the birth of each of her children. Every two years she spent two weeks in the hospital. Every two

`

years. Yes, there was a difference in age of about two years between each of my brothers and sisters. But I was six, not two, when Evelyn was born. My mother was almost forty. In those days, it was unusual for women to give birth at that age. Perhaps my mother wore such a big white apron because she was ashamed. Perhaps she had been hiding after all, just as I had thought when I first searched for her, many years ago.

Two weeks in the hospital. So, that was the amount of time she was away, I finally learned. Two weeks? When my mother was gone, time stopped and had neither beginning nor end. But it was only two weeks. Only two weeks.

4

DON'T GO TO HIRSHMAN'S DRUGSTORE

We filled all of our prescriptions at Hirshman's Drugstore. It was just a block away on the corner of Monroe and Presbury Streets, catty-corner from Shearer's grocery store. I liked going to Hirshman's. It was a very special drug store. In the window were large glass globes filled with red and blue liquids. They looked very mysterious. There were also big marble jars with grinding sticks on display. All the words on the jars were in Latin.

When you went inside the drugstore, the first thing you noticed was the way the store smelled. It was a special smell, not unpleasant and very different from the way our house smelled. Hirshman's smell was clean; it was how clean things were supposed to smell. It was cool. It was a mixture of hospital and doctor's office smells. That smell always told me I was in a place that was very medical.

A small soda fountain gleamed to the right as you entered the store. The countertop was made of marble and there were three large stools with padded leather seats. The stools were hard to climb onto, but brought you to the height of the counter. Sometimes, when I went to Hirshman's, I would have an ice cream soda made in a special tall glass.

Beyond the soda fountain were long, glass cases, containing articles of special importance for every bodily mishap or function you could imagine. There were jars of Vaseline, bottles of Mercurochrome, iodine, and Argyrol, an awful-tasting medicine that my mother dripped into my nose when I had a cold. Bandages of various sizes, lengths, and materials were on another shelf, along with rolls of adhesive tape. Of course, there was a

`

display of scary enema bags in bright red colors. The bags had long tubes capped with nozzles of various shapes to fit every anatomical variation of you-know- what.

Finally, at the far end of the store, Mr. Hirshman himself held forth in his clean, crisp white coat. He filled prescriptions and, when they were ready, he rolled out just the correct length of paper, tore it off cleanly and neatly, and began the process of wrapping up the medicine. I watched in awe as he folded each side of the paper around the filled prescription, making sure the ends of the paper were neat, and finally secured the wrapping with just the right length of Scotch tape.

One day, my mother called me into her room. There was something special that she wanted me to do for her. She handed me a small, folded piece of paper. "There is a Read's drugstore on North Avenue and Druid Hill Avenue. Take this with you. Just give this to the pharmacist. He will know

`

what to give you. But don't go to Hirshman's drugstore," she said. I was puzzled. I couldn't understand why I was to go to the other drugstore. It was much farther away, by at least five blocks. Hirshman's was just down the street. That didn't matter. I set off as I was told.

I left the house and headed up Monroe Street in the direction opposite of Hirshman's. As I walked, I kept searching for an answer. Why was I going to another drug store? I could not contain my curiosity. Perhaps there might be an answer if I unfolded the paper to see what my mother had written. I struggled with myself, knowing that I would be doing something terribly wrong if I looked. I was told to just hand the paper to the pharmacist. Maybe, maybe if I just glanced at the writing, it wouldn't count. I could just look for a second. Should I or shouldn't I? I was getting close to my destination so there was little time left. Finally, I gave in

`

and carefully undid the fold in the paper so I could read the forbidden message.

I did not understand. My mother had carefully printed out two words: ORTHOGYNOL JELLY. What did that mean? Why do you get jelly from a drugstore? I did not have words to think about it. The thoughts that came to my mind were not connected with my mother. I knew that what my mother wanted from the drug store had something to do with *it* but at the same time there was no way I could connect *it* with my mother. I knew that I wasn't supposed to know, but somehow I knew and I didn't know at the same time. I carried out the rest of my mission in a state of disbelief and bewilderment.

Read's Drugstore was large and busy. It didn't smell like Hirshman's. It smelled like a store. There were counters filled with lots of things that didn't have anything to do with a drug store. There were displays of bathing caps, cigarette lighters, beach

`

toys, magazines, cleaning supplies, calendars, picture frames—all sorts of things that would never be found at Hirshman's. I went past all of them to the prescription counter. People were in line and I waited until it was my turn.

When the man behind the counter asked me what I wanted, I felt embarrassed. I couldn't say anything. I just handed him the folded piece of paper. He read it, disappeared behind lots of big shelves filled with little boxes and bottles. He came back with a small rectangular, cardboard box. Unlike Mr. Hirshman who would have wrapped it neatly, the druggist just slipped the box into a small bag and gave it to me. I paid for it with the money my mother had given me. I carried the mysterious package home and handed it to my mother. I had trouble looking at my mother. She thanked me.

My mother didn't want Mr. Hirshman to know. Certainly I was not to know. But I do

`

know that I went to the other drugstore
after my younger sister Evelyn was born
and that it had something to do with my
not having any more brothers or sisters.

5

TIME FOR SCHOOL

We were inseparable. My sister Libbye was two years older. I wanted to be wherever she was. I was glued to her. I was attached, bonded, connected, involved, coupled, and enamored of her. We were often taken on

`

walks by Mozella, a black woman who looked after us when my father worked in the bakery and my mother worked in the store. Our older siblings were already in school so Libbye and I spent much of our time together.

One day, something happened on our walk that threatened that cherished togetherness. We headed down Monroe Street as usual, but instead of turning right on Baker Street, which would have taken us to Easterwood Park, we turned left. It was a new route. Why were we going a different way? We came to a big building. Why are we stopping here? It was a school. We went inside. I looked around, but suddenly, Libbye wasn't with me anymore. Where had she gone?

Mozella took me by the hand and led me outside. I want to stay with Libbye, I protested. No, Libbye is going to school.... I want to go to school.... You're not old enough.

`

My words didn't seem to matter. It became clear that Libbye was going to stay at school and I was going to go home. I could not believe what was happening. What would I do without Libbye? I dragged my feet. Mozella pulled harder. It was hopeless.

Bereft, I sobbed. I cried. I pleaded. I bargained. I begged. Please let me go to school with Libbye. Please. Please. Mozella had little to say. I didn't want to go home without Libbye. I left behind a trail of tears. I choked and could hardly breathe. Somehow, finally I did stop crying. But my sadness never went away. Libbye had gone to school.

6

MY JEWISH EDUCATION

My Jewish education was complete in every respect. It began in a formal sense when I was about eight. My father had decided it was time for me to attend *cheder,* the Hebrew school connected with our shul. I was to go there every day after school. The cheder was located in a building next to the synagogue. There was a large meeting room on the ground floor and a flight of stairs led to the rooms set aside for teaching on the second floor. The building was in disrepair and my memories of it are mainly connected with its smell. It was dank, heavy, and redolent of sweat and the gaseous odor of boys. The bathroom reeked of stale urine and unflushed toilets.

Rabbi Rubin presided over the class. He was one of the most frightening men I

`

remember from my childhood. He insisted on complete submission to his authority and control. We were initially taught the Hebrew alphabet, which we recited in a rote way in response to Mr. Rubin's direction. At some point, we were ready to read Hebrew and were given texts that we read aloud. Advanced teaching methods were used: drill, repetition, reciting in unison, chanting at a tempo defined by the conductor's baton, and a ruler, wielded energetically by Mr. Rubin in crisp, martial cadence. I recall learning the meaning of only a few words. Most of what we read was not translated and neither my fellow classmates nor I had any idea of what we were reading. We learned to read without understanding.

However, what we were taught and did learn to understand clearly was the power of the rabbi, Mr. Rubin. He ruled with an iron fist. If anyone spoke out of turn, there was a sharp whack across the knuckles with a ruler. If anyone was caught

`

throwing spitballs, the punishment was worse: Mr. Rubin would grab the offender by the collar, lift him from the seat and smack him across the back of his head. More severe infractions were punished by being shoved against the wall. I do remember one boy being thrown down the stairs as we were leaving the building. I was never clear about what he had done wrong but it must have been something magnificently defiant.

If I attended an orthodox cheder to satisfy my father's religious requirements for me, then I also attended a Reform Sunday school to satisfy my mother's. So, during the week I went to cheder and on Sundays I was sent to the Madison Avenue Synagogue for even more religious education. I believe that my mother expressed her wish to become more American and perhaps less like other eastern European Jews by connecting with this Reform synagogue. It was in a neighborhood populated mostly by

`

German Jews, the elite Jews of Baltimore. Classes were conducted in English so that I actually learned something about Jewish history, the holidays, and Jewish rituals.

Because I had already learned to read Hebrew in cheder, I received an unexpected bonus. Much to my delight, I was excused from Hebrew classes at Sunday school and allowed free range in the school library for one hour. For some reason, the library contained the whole of the *Oz* series, so I became as familiar with Dorothy, Auntie Em, Toto, Munchkins, and the Tin Man as I was with matters Judaic.

There was another ritual that was also observed religiously. Each fall, I had a new suit made for me to wear when attending Rosh Hashanah and Yom Kippur services. My Uncle Jake, who had broken off from a partnership with my father in the bakery business, became a clothing manufacturer. His shop occupied a floor in a large building on Pratt Street in downtown

`

Baltimore. Told how to get to Uncle Jake's by streetcar, I dutifully made my way by public transportation to his place of business. A rickety elevator took me to his floor.

My uncle greeted me and promptly set about making all the measurements for a new suit. The suit was produced within a few days and, of course, fit me perfectly. There was a major flaw, however. For reasons I never understood, the suit was always made of rough, heavy tweed, even though the High Holy Days always seemed to happen during warm Indian summers. When I was fully clad in my knickers, long socks, and jacket, I felt encased in a blanket of rough sandpaper and barbed wire. I itched all over and was never comfortable. My new clothes added to the agony of attending shul.

My father would purchase a row of seats at one side of the synagogue. He occupied the seat at the end of the row so there was no escape. My brothers and I were trapped. Services were conducted entirely in Hebrew and I had no understanding of their meaning. I stood when everyone else did, weaved and bobbed as prayers were mumbled, and sat down when everyone else did. I popped up and down like a robot. The hours I spent in shul seemed like an eternity. It was tedious and boring beyond anything imaginable. I searched the upper balcony longingly for my mother, who would sometimes appear there with her sister, my Aunt Katie.

The notion of separation of church and state somehow had not yet found its way to Baltimore. At school, we recited biblical verses every day just before pledging allegiance to the flag. As Christmas approached, we sang carols at every opportunity. Like all of my Jewish friends, I learned to hold my lips tight and not to say the word "Christ" when it appeared in one of the carols. As a special treat, our teachers gave us Christmas candy canes

`

before we set out for the Christmas holiday. At the Robert E. Lee Junior High School (or more familiarly, P.S. 49) I was chosen to sing at a special Christmas program. It was considered a great honor. I had a great pre-pubertal soprano voice. To this day, I still love to sing Christmas carols.

Christmas was everywhere. Not much was made of
Hanukah. There were no public menorahs but we did light one at home. We were given Hanukah *gelt*—
"chocolate money"—but that was it. No gifts. I suffered from a common malady among Jewish children: Christmas envy. Somehow, my mother must have understood that. When I was nine or ten, I had a transforming religious experience.

On Christmas Eve, I asked my mother if I could hang a Christmas stocking. (I must have known that gifts were out of the question so I aimed my sights low.) To my amazement, she agreed. I hung the biggest sock I could find at the foot of my bed. My mother did not disappoint me. In the morning, my sock was brimming with excesses of Hershey candy kisses, each wrapped in silver foil with its paper tail protruding. How delicious! So Jews could celebrate Christmas after all!

As my Bar Mitzvah approached, it became painfully clear that I was incapable of learning the Torah portion I was to read. For inexplicable reasons, I was severely handicapped in learning Hebrew. How could that be? In no other area of my education did such a disability exist. I was totally unaware of the subtle rebellion that was taking place. Fortunately, it also remained hidden from my father, who treated my learning disability as merely a slight impediment, easily remedied. My therapy was to undertake individual instruction at the hands of yet another rabbi. I was sent to another synagogue for special tutoring. Finally, I must have

`

realized the futility of my pseudo-stupidity. I yielded to the relentless pressure and readied myself for my Bar Mitzvah.

In preparation for my Bar Mitzvah I was also taught to lay *tefillin,* or phylacteries, on long leather straps, wrapped around the forearm and head. A small box attached to the straps contained verses from the Torah. There was a prescribed way of wrapping tefillin and I was taught prayers that accompanied this ritual. I also had to wear *tzitzit* under my shirt. Tzitit is a short piece of clothing made like a jacket with hanging fringes that had some religious meaning never explained to me.

My Bar Mitzvah was a far cry from the lavish celebrations of today. I took my place on the *bima,* the raised platform in front of the ark where Torahs are stored. Then a Torah on a big stand was unfurled and my place marked with a silver pointer held by the rabbi. I struggled through my portion. Reading was especially difficult for me because Hebrew in the Torah is written only with consonants and no vowels. I had never really memorized my portion and was mostly winging it. I was painfully slow but I finally managed to get through it. At the end of the ceremony I was presented with an inscribed silver cup, a gift from the synagogue. After services, the men adjourned to the basement where they ate globs of herring washed down with quick gulps of whiskey, called *schnapps*. There was a lunch at home for my parents' friends, and card tables were set up in the living room to accommodate everyone. I felt superfluous. But it was over and I was relieved.

My father was president of the synagogue. Even though I had rejected much of what I had been exposed to about religion, I had always assumed that since my father was religiously observant, he actually believed in the Jewish religion. Sometimes I would sit quietly in the kitchen when family would gather there so that I could absorb

`

the conversations that took place. My father made fun of religion and of the relatives who believed in it. He boasted about how little he really cared about religion. For me, religious observance was an extension of my father. The lesson I had learned at cheder—blind obedience to authority through fear and physical and psychological abuse—was the same lesson in hypocrisy I had already learned at home.

After my Bar Mitzvah I knew I had come to the end of meeting my father's requirements for my religious indoctrination. I had graduated. My Jewish education was complete.

7

STRICTLY KOSHER

You didn't just observe the rules of kosher. You *kept* kosher. Jews kept kosher. Non-Jews did not keep kosher. We kept kosher.

We lived in a neighborhood of row houses that was mostly Jewish. My mother shopped only at kosher stores and sometimes, bought chickens from a *shochet,* a butcher who slaughtered in the manner proscribed by kosher laws. We ate only kosher food. Kosher chickens were brought home and plucked, feather-by-feather. Fish was ground in a hand-operated machine attached to the edge of the kitchen counter and transformed into gefilte fish. No shellfish. No crabs. Only fish with scales were considered kosher.

Jewish food abounded: potato *latkes*—"pancakes"—at Hanukah, blintzes, brisket,

60

boiled tongue with sweet and sour sauce, *luchshen kugel* (it would lose its *tam,* or "flavor" if called noodle pudding), and *tsimmes*—a mixture of sweet potatoes, carrots, prunes, and from what I could tell, anything else that could be thrown into the pot. (Hence, the expression "to make a tsimmes" out of something means to enlarge or embellish it.) There were kosher grocery stores and a kosher butcher shop within a block of our house. Every particle of food that entered the house was kosher. All other foods were not kosher. They were called *trayf.* Trayf was very bad.

Keeping kosher also meant that we separated dairy and meat and had separate utensils and dishes for each: *flayshig* for meat and *milchik* for milk. Never the twain shall meet. There was never butter on the table when meat was served. Nor was milk or cream added to coffee if meat had been served. We even had separate dishes for *Pesach,* Passover. They were stored in an upstairs closet and each year were hauled out and used only during the eight days of Pesach. Of course, there were milchik and flayshig dishes for Pesach as well as for everyday use, so altogether the household operated with four distinct sets of dishes and silverware.

Early in its history, the bakery was shut down for *Shabbes,* the Sabbath, from Friday night until sundown on Saturday. Women brought casseroles or stews to the bakery at the end of the day on Friday, which were then placed in the oven. Although the oven was shut down, it cooled gradually, so that by the next day the dishes had baked sufficiently to be ready for lunch when families returned from shul on Shabbes. No one could be accused of violating the laws of Shabbes. The oven had not been turned on. No work had been performed.

Sometimes on summer Sunday afternoons, we would pile into our car and head for *the shore.* My father belonged to something called the Ritchie Club (named after a Maryland governor) and the club owned property on Chesapeake Bay. When we arrived, we jumped out of our car and ran behind one of the shacks to change into our bathing suits.

One Sunday, Uncle Jake Rodbell was with us. I told him I was embarrassed and afraid some of the girls might see me naked. He explained that I didn't have to worry, "If they haven't seen *it*, they won't know what *it* is and if they have already seen *it*, they won't be surprised." That was of enormous relief to me.

After we put on our bathing suits, we ran into the bay and cooled ourselves in the tepid, shallow waters. When we came out, we showered, dried ourselves, and got ready to eat. One afternoon, when I was about nine, I noticed that something different was set out for dinner. What was going on? Wooden picnic tables had been covered with newspaper and then huge

`

basketfuls of red, steamed crabs were dumped out on top. I hesitated. Weren't crabs trayf, non-kosher? And besides, with such hard shells, how could you eat them? I looked toward my father. He certainly wasn't going to eat any. And I would not make that mistake.

But my father had already picked out one of the largest of the crabs and, armed with a wooden mallet, nutcracker, and small pick had begun attacking his prey with a vengeance. I watched my Uncle Jake, who sat next to me. From him I learned the art of releasing the succulent white crab meat from its shell. Lift the hinge, here, I was told. Break the shell in half. Tear off the claws. Don't eat the gills. Scrape away all this other stuff. Crack open the big claws. Use the pick to scrape out the meat. Suck the little claws. Throw the shells here. Use the paper towels to wipe your mouth and hands. We hardly spoke. We were too busy with the serious business at hand. What an orgy of unfettered appetite for such forbidden fruit.

The shells, claws, gills, and green stuff piled up on the table. What a mess. My mouth burned with the seasoning. I drank lots of Coke from funny green bottles, shaped like Mae West. All of the grown-ups drank lots of beer. My father was not angry. He was having a good time. I could relax. He loved hard-shell crabs. It was fun.

When I was 14, we moved from Monroe Street to Liberty Heights Avenue. No row houses here. Now a spacious lawn separated us from our neighbor. There were large shade trees, a grape arbor, apple trees, and finally, a place for a garden. We no longer had to borrow dirt from Mrs. Brinkley, our neighbor on Monroe Street, to grow plants. When we left our old house, I think my parents left behind a working class neighborhood and could now feel part of middle class America. They also left behind another

`

remnant of their kosher past: the dishes that separated milk from meat and also defined them as part of Orthodoxy. Now, we had only one set of dishes, not four. We now lived in Forest Park.

Another change took place. We no longer had to travel to the shore to enjoy hard-shell crabs. We ate them, but never inside the house. That would have been going too far. Somehow, as long as they were not in the house, technically we still maintained a kosher home. We had a patio on which to have crab feasts, another mark of having made it. We had moved up and out of the more crowded "ghettoish" Monroe Street neighborhood.

Finally, the last encroachment on the strict rules of keeping kosher took place. My mother loved crab cakes. Making crab cakes did not involve bringing hard-shell crabs into the home, since the crabmeat, already separated from its shells, was in cans. Her crab cakes were delicate works

`

of culinary art, made with large lumps of back-fin crabmeat. Since the hard shells of the crabs were not brought inside, we were somehow still keeping kosher. We were only eating the crabmeat. No shells contaminated the house.

Some rules had to be maintained. Milk and meat never appeared together at the same meal. One imperative remained inviolate: we never ate ham or bacon. After all, we were strictly kosher.

8

SKATING ON THIN ICE

My father was in a good mood. That was ominous. We had been driving together for fifteen minutes. Not a word was exchanged, but somehow I could feel he was not angry with me. I braced myself when finally he broke the silence. "Earle," he began in his thick Jewish accent, "I'm sending you to school; you'll learn ice skate." Oh my God, I thought, that's it. He's figured out that I had been ice skating on Sunday mornings rather than working in the store. Now I see. He's playing with me. He's teasing. Has he found out? What should I do? Should I tell him the truth? Would that be worse? My head pounding, heart thumping, and barely able to breathe, I decided to make a full confession and hope for the best.

`

I took a deep breath. "Pop, I'm sorry. I already know how to ice skate. I know I should have stayed home to work in the store on Sundays, but I did sometimes go to Carlin's ice-skating rink. I taught myself to skate. I know I'm supposed to help in the store. I'm sorry. I should have stayed home. I don't have to take skating lessons. I'm sorry. I know the store is busy on Sundays. I'm sorry. I shouldn't have gone skating. I'm sorry. I promise I won't do that any more. I'm sorry. I'm really sorry." I blabbered on and on. He said nothing. Finally he repeated, "No, you don' understand. I'm sending you to school. You'll learn ice cake!"

"Ice cake?" I thought. Whatever that meant, I knew he wasn't going to let me have it for ice-skating on Sunday mornings. I was safe. I would do whatever he said to escape. I would learn the details later. Right now, I could relax. But what did he mean by "ice cake?"

`

In time, I learned that my father had decided that I would attend a cake decorating school every afternoon for the next two months. The school traveled from city to city and was occupying a suite of rooms at the Hotel Rennert, a historic hotel wedged between Saratoga and Liberty Streets in downtown Baltimore. So, at the age of 12, I was enrolled as the youngest member of the class. Other bakeries had sent emissaries, mostly men in their forties or fifties, to learn this arcane art along with me.

On the day I began my new career, I awoke with a sick stomach. My mother had written out for me the directions from my junior high school, P.S. 49, to the hotel. I tucked away the slip of paper in my Latin book. All day, I dreaded the end of school. When it came, I slipped out quickly and silently ahead of my schoolmates, hoping they wouldn't notice that I was not going home with them as usual. I walked to Charles Street, boarded a bus, got off at

`

Saratoga and found my way to the hotel, taking shorter and shorter steps to delay the inevitable. But in an instant, I was in the hotel and given directions to the suite that had been taken over by the decorating school.

It was strange. The furniture in the rooms had been replaced with tables and small mixing machines in which icing was made. The room was brightly lit and smelled of powdered sugar. When I entered I felt embarrassed by the gaze of the older men in the class. I felt as if my face was on fire. I mumbled my name. I was recognized as "one of the Silber boys." I found a place to hide my books and was given an apron, much too large, so that it had to be folded in half to fit. I found a place in the back of the room and tried to be invisible.

The course began with the fundamentals of icing, introduction to borders, floral arrangements (including basics of leaves, stems, and clusters), flower creation (roses, carnations, lilies of the valley, forget-me-nots, chrysanthemums), then moved on to Greek columns, doves, grapes, advanced borders, marzipan, calligraphy, and ornamentation. We learned to use various metal tips in conical tubes to create different designs out of icing. There were even sessions on color. I leaned the magic of creating a vast spectrum of color from only three basic vegetable dyes of red, blue, and yellow.

We moved progressively through decorating simple birthday cakes, shower cakes (a half-opened umbrella made of marzipan), bar mitzvah cakes (complete with ten commandment tablets), Thanksgiving cakes (with more marzipan shaped into apples, pears, pineapples, peaches, oranges, and bananas cascading out of a cornucopia), and finally each of us was allowed to design our own wedding cake. Mine was a baroque masterpiece of three tiers replete with all manner of elaborate borders, birds, garlands of

`

grapes, roses, columns entwined with flowers, capped with a bride and groom in loving embrace, supported by an ornate pedestal under a little tent that was called a "chuppa." In the world of pastry bakers, it was comparable to completing a Ph.D. thesis. I was now a certified cake decorator and sadly for me, that became my new job in the bakery.

Of course, my career in ice-skating came to an abrupt halt. Instead, my Sundays and evenings were often occupied with decorating the never-ending stream of cakes awaiting my newly acquired skill. Sometimes I had to work at night. The kitchen table was cleared to make room for all of the paraphernalia I needed: bowls of icing, coloring dyes, spatulas, ornaments, and metal tips of every kind for flowers and borders. Wedding cakes were especially difficult and took lots of time. I would grow exhausted. During all of this, I was determined not to fall behind in my schoolwork and I sometimes stayed up late

`

into the night ensuring that all of my homework was done on time. My mother stayed up with me and offered some comfort. I took consolation in realizing that I had escaped a far greater punishment: my father's wrath. I knew I had been skating on thin ice.

9

CHILD LABOR

By the time child labor laws were enacted under FDR in 1938, it was too late to protect most of my siblings and me. The law exempted children who worked on family-owned farms but did not mention family-owned bakeries. From an early age,

`

we were expected to work in the bakery and we each had rather specific jobs. My first began when I was about 10.

When my parents were away, the task of looking after the bakery was assigned to those of us who were at home. Sometimes, my sister Libbye, all of 12, took care of checking the receipts in the main store on Monroe Street. I was her assistant. She would empty the cash register and tear off the record of all the sales that had been rung up. One of the rooms on the second floor of our house served as an office, where business transactions took place. Libbye brought her financial items to this room, where she and I worked at a desk together. My job was to help her count the money. We added up the cash and made sure it corresponded to the sales that had been registered. Libbye made up a bank deposit slip, which was placed in a small bag with the cash. For reasons that were not clear to me then, we were told to put aside some of the money, maybe $20 or so, which went into the safe.

After the cash was tallied up and secured, off I went to the local bank to make the deposit. I headed up Monroe Street, turned right on North Avenue and walked a few blocks to the corner of Druid Hill Avenue, where I entered the Union Trust Company Bank. I stood in line and presented my bundle to the bank clerk, who counted it up and then stamped the deposit slip and handed it back to me. I felt very important.

By age 11, there were more expectations. On Saturday mornings, I took over the operation of a doughnut machine, installed in the corner of the store. The machine was a Rube Goldberg contraption. Batter was loaded into a large cylinder that extruded circles of dough, which dropped into hot sizzling and bubbling cooking oil. Each doughnut was in its own compartment and moved in an arc around the machine to the midpoint, where it was flipped over. It

`

continued on its journey as it was cooked to perfection, and arrived at another device that ejected the completed doughnut out of the machine. Of course, anything could go wrong and I was assigned the task of monitoring this fascinating machine. As the doughnuts rolled down from the machine, I arranged them neatly on a tray.

My next bigger job was called "waiting on the store." Whenever there was a surfeit of customers waiting to be served, I was sent in to help out. I learned the price of everything in the bakery and transacted the sale of bread, rolls, pies, cakes, éclairs, strawberry shortcake, Napoleons, Charlotte Russes, Hamantashen, and cookies. I was an essentially shy child, so this was not easy for me. I was not comfortable behind the counter, but I did learn to smile when I didn't feel like smiling. Learning to figure out the costs of each purchase improved my math skills, but that did not seem like an advantage at the time. I remember particular customers.

`

An elderly man would ask for a special kind of bread, called gluten bread. His breath had a peculiar odor. I had already learned, before going to medical school, that this was a sign of diabetes.

Working in the store was not restricted to the main store on Monroe Street. Sometimes, I was taken in one of the trucks to a branch store that required extra help. I remember working in the store on Garrison Avenue in a section of Baltimore called Forest Park. Some of my classmates from junior high school would come in with their parents. I was deeply embarrassed when I had to wait on them. I wished I could hide, or better yet, disappear entirely.

At other times, I worked at the Silber's Bakery stall at Lexington Market. That was quite different. The stall was located near the center of the market and was surrounded by other stands with displays of every kind of food imaginable: cheese,

`

meat, shellfish, fresh corn, tomatoes, string beans, onions, candy, pears, apples, pasta, oranges, milk, ham, fish, baloney, pickles, and blocks of my favorite confection: halavah.

People sat at a counter on high stools and consumed freshly shucked raw oysters. The market seemed to be in constant motion, like a swarm of bees. It was always busy. People pushed their way through the narrow aisles carrying large shopping bags brimming with purchases, some from Hochschild-Kohn and Hutzler's, two nearby department stores. There was a constant buzzing noise made up of police whistles, automobiles, buses, clanging street cars, screeching brakes, crates being dropped, workmen shouting to one another, and vendors yelling to attract customers. Outside the market, garbage piled up in ever-growing mountains as the day wore on. An occasional rat scurried underfoot.

`

At Christmas time, I had a new job in the bakery: decorating the front window of the store. No Christmas ornaments. The décor did not include any direct reference to anything religious. I draped garlands of red and green crepe paper across the window. From these I hung icicles made of tinsel. Then a good dusting of white artificial snow and the window was transformed into a veritable winter wonderland. For a final touch I unfolded paper bells (not really church bells) and placed them discreetly in the corners of the window. I added a few sprinkles of snow for good measure.

A special, new holiday item appeared in the bakery: gingerbread cut-out cookies. Not just any gingerbread. To these figures were pasted a picturesque, old- fashioned Victorian image of St. Nicholas, not to be confused with Santa Claus. He had a grey beard and carried a bag of toys slung over his back. He was, after all, the saint who looked after children. I used some of these to complete my window display. The bakery had come a long way from its early kosher days.

During the summers, I rode along on the trucks that delivered goods to all of the branch stores. Dave Gordon was my mentor, telling me what was to be taken into each of the stores. He was also an unintentional mentor in another part of life that was never spoken about at home: sex. Sometimes another helper went along. I listened with riveted attention to their jokes and accounts of their erotic escapades. They were the source of very informative and vital information about which of the sales girls did really bad things and who did it with them.

The truck stopped at each of the stores: first, along North Avenue to Walbrook Junction, then out Garrison Avenue to the store in Forest Park, on to the store near the Pimlico race track on Park Heights Avenue, and sometimes on the return

`

route, stopping at a small grocery store run by a relative with the odd name of Lily Tiger. There was another run in the opposite direction on North Avenue to a store near Eutaw Place. These were highly educational days for a twelve-year-old boy.

Of course, my most acclaimed work was as the bakery cake decorator. I have already recounted how that came about. Once I became a certified cake decorator, I was pressed into service filling orders for birthday cakes, shower cakes, Bar Mitzvah cakes, anniversary cakes, Thanksgiving cakes, wedding cakes, and any other special order cakes. It was something of a novelty at first and I could use my imagination to some extent in creating each masterpiece. But very soon, the charm wore off and the work gradually drifted into drudgery and boredom. I would have preferred playing with my friends, listening to music or reading. My mother appreciated what I was feeling and, thankfully, she would stay with me at nights when I was still at work to meet a deadline for a cake to be delivered the next day. Later in my life, I resurrected my decorating skills with more pleasure in designing and executing birthday cakes for my children and grandchildren. It was by no means a total loss.

By age thirteen, a work ethic had been deeply entrenched in my personality. I even thought about work I could do on my own. I learned from my friend, Herbie Adler, that by working for one of the neighborhood movie theatres, it was possible to go to the movies without paying. All you had to do was deliver circulars describing the weekly movie schedule. Wow! What an opportunity.

Without hesitation, I walked to the Metropolitan Theatre, the Met, on North Avenue. I asked to speak to the manager and told him I would like to deliver circulars. He agreed, gave me a packet, and confirmed the deal: from then on, I could

`

see movies free of charge. I could hardly wait to tell my father. I was sure he would be pleased at my initiative. Besides, it would save him money. When I arrived home, bursting with pride, I explained to my father what I had arranged with the manager of the movie house. I would no longer have to ask for money to go to the movies.

I should have known. My father was furious. He exploded. I showed him the circulars. He threw them in the trash. Work was what I did for the bakery. If I had time to give out circulars, I had time to work in the bakery. How could I be so stupid not to understand that? He was in a rage. I had learned not to cry when he became abusive. I turned and left the room. I blamed myself, not for what I had done, but for thinking that this time, my father would be proud of me.

Child labor laws in my family did not apply to work connected with the bakery. There

`

was, however, a strict prohibition against a
child working somewhere else.

10

THE PRICE OF ADMISSION

I had to hurry to keep up with my father. He told me that I should get ready to leave right away because he was taking me to my first lacrosse game. But before we could leave, he had to stop in to the bakery. He began to fill two large paper bags with anything he could reach: loaves of rye bread, Kaiser rolls, chocolate drop cookies, sticky pecan buns, cupcakes, peach cakes, and cream-filled doughnuts. I couldn't understand what bags filled with Silber's Bakery's delicacies had to do with lacrosse. I knew better than to ask. I would find out soon enough. We loaded the bags into the back seat of the car and finally were on our way. We turned left from Westwood Avenue onto Monroe Street and headed south.

We passed block after block of row houses. Soon the neighborhood changed and there

`

were more garages, warehouses, and empty lots. Monroe Street became Route One, which was the main thoroughfare connecting Baltimore and Washington. It was a wide, three-lane road and we drove past open fields, punctuated with bright yellow forsythia bushes that were just coming into bloom. My father drove slowly and carefully, with both hands on the wheel. After what seemed a very long time, probably less than two hours, we came to College Park where my brother Sam was attending the University of Maryland. I was very excited when my father told me that we were going to see him play lacrosse.

When we arrived, my father took both of the bags from the car and we joined a large crowd of people making their way to the main entrance of a huge stadium. There was a booth where tickets were being sold, but my father pushed me ahead and didn't stop. We had no tickets. How would we get in?

We merged into a line of college students, teachers, parents, and friends and became part of a crush of people pushing us up to the ticket collector. Instead of presenting tickets, my father shoved the bags under his nose. My father, in his Yiddish accent, explained, "Ve're bringing buns for de players." The ticket collector looked puzzled. The crowd surged behind us and pushed us into the stadium before the ticket collector really knew what had happened. It was too late for him to do anything but shrug his shoulders. We headed for the locker room.

Someone at the entrance who seemed to recognize him greeted my father. "Buns for de players," my father repeated and handed over the two bags brimming with bakery goods. After depositing the bags, we turned back toward the stands. My father spotted some empty seats and we made our way to them and sat down to enjoy the game.

`

I found a program on the seat next to me, opened it, and saw a picture of the Maryland team. There was Sam, standing in the back row, holding a long lacrosse stick by his side. He looked very big and strong. I found his name listed among the players. The position he played was called Cover Point.

The game began. My eyes were fixed only on one of the players: Sam. I saw him knock the ball from his opponent's lacrosse stick, scoop it up, run behind the goal, cradle the ball in his stick, lift his stick over his shoulder, and then catapult the ball far into the air halfway down the field to one of the Maryland attack players. Within a minute, the player passed the ball to another player, who scored a goal. Everyone stood up at the same time and cheered: "Yeah Silber!" I cheered too. My heart burst with pride. I was Sam's brother. Maryland won the game.

`

After the game, we went back to the locker room. When we entered, we were met with a warm cloud of steam that smelled of sweat All of the players were yelling, joking, sweating, pulling off shirts, untying shoes, sliding off shorts, snapping towels, taking showers, taking off shoulder guards, throwing uniforms in piles, clapping each other on the back, putting on street clothes, making lots of noise, and having a good time. I felt I had been allowed into a very special place. Sam gave me a big hug.

It had been a glorious afternoon, one that I always remembered because it was so rare. I had actually spent time alone with my father. He was not angry. Going to the game was worth any price that I could imagine. But my father knew the price of admission: two bags of Silber's Bakery goods.

11

SECRET INGREDIENT

Silber's peach cakes were one of the
bakery's specialties. They were in great
demand during the summer months when
families poured into the stores and carried
away bags filled to overflowing with bread,
rolls, buns, pies, cookies, and peach cakes
to take with them to picnics and nearby
beaches. When they were available, peach

`

cakes sold out in a hurry. Why? What made them so delicious and sought after? What was the secret ingredient?

I learned the answer on an excursion with my father that took us to Baltimore's waterfront. That day was different from most days I spent with my father. Just as he had been at the lacrosse game, he was in a good mood. He wasn't angry.

My father drove downtown, past Hochschild-Kohn's department store, past the Bromo-Seltzer Tower, past Lombard Street to Pratt Street. It was so early in the morning that there were still parking places available. My father parked the car, and we walked toward the waterfront.

Excursion boats, ferries, motor launches, and boats laden with machinery, huge crates, bundles, bananas, and other tropical fruit, all were anchored, bobbing gently, moored to piers that jutted out into the Baltimore harbor. The water was coated with oil, brown with waste, garbage, and empty cans. We passed stall after stall where produce was being unloaded. The gutters of Pratt Street were filled with garbage. The stench of rotting apples, peaches, wilted lettuce, banana peels, and all manner of rejected fruit and vegetables was almost sickening, yet sweet-smelling at the same time. No one seemed to care about the number and size of the rats that scurried about, foraging on the plentiful supply of food.

My father knew which stalls sold peaches. We stopped at the first. One of the men inside brought out a basket and bent back the wires holding the top to display his wares. My father picked up one of the peaches. Without saying a word, he took a big bite out of the peach. After a brief moment of tasting, my father stepped toward the curb, threw his head back, inhaled deeply, took aim and spat the remaining pulp right into the gutter. The rest of the peach followed. We went from

`

stall to stall, where the same ritual was performed.

Peach after peach was bitten into, tasted, spit out, and discarded. Finally, my father bit into a peach he liked. He had found the right stall. But then, since he was buying a number of baskets, a peach in each basket had to be tasted. One by one, he selected nine baskets. Then the bargaining over the price began.

The first price was of course rejected. In his heavily accented English, my father made it clear that the price for nine should make for a reduction in the cost per basket. My father was very quick with numbers, and I was impressed that without pencil and paper, he multiplied and divided prices rapidly, never losing a beat in his duel with the produce man. A final price was agreed upon. The nine baskets were set aside. My father instructed me to stay with the peaches he had selected to make sure no other ones were substituted while he went for the car.

`

I stood guard. I pretended not to see the rats. I began to be worried and it seemed a long time before my father returned. I stopped being nervous when I saw my father drive up and park in front of the stall. My father and I then loaded the baskets onto the back seat and floor of the car. My father seemed pleased. As we drove back through the now crowded streets, we didn't say anything to each other. That was an enormous relief. Nothing unpleasant happened on the way home.

We unloaded the peaches and carried each basket from the car, through the bakery shipping room into our kitchen. My mother, Mozella, and Mary began cutting them into slices. Expecting the arrival of peaches, Charlie Tormollen, the head baker, had been working on preparing the dough for the peach cakes. Circular pieces of dough had been stuffed into greased round pans. Six pans on each tray were brought into the kitchen to receive their ample supply of fruit.

Peaches were arranged in neat little circles on the dough in each pan. As the trays were finished, more helpers came into the kitchen to retrieve them and take them back into the bakery. Trays of unbaked cakes were slipped into the oven on long paddles. When ready, they were retrieved, brought into the shipping room and then distributed to the main store and branch stores where customers were eagerly awaiting the arrival of Silber's famous peach cakes.

The secret ingredient of the peach cakes was very obvious to me: it was my father's trained palate. He not only knew where to find the right peaches, he also knew how to find just the right ones: ripe, but not overripe; sweet; juicy, but not soggy. Just as a good wine taster never swallows the wine, my father never swallowed any of

`

the bites of peaches he tasted. His discerning judgment was the secret.

But another secret remains. What was the ingredient that made it possible for me to spend a pleasant day with my father? There were so few days like that one that it has remained very special and fixed in my memory. Why was my father in a good mood? Why was this day different from all other days? That remains a mystery.

12

A RAISIN IN THE BUN

I noticed the lady standing in the back of the counter. She looked nervous. She didn't push ahead of anyone but waited until she was the last customer in the store. She was clutching a bag. When the salesgirl asked what she would like, she answered in a tiny voice. She wanted to meet with Mr. Silber. Ike Silber? Yes, the owner, Ike Silber. Just a minute. The salesgirl went into the bakery where my father was working and told him that someone wanted to talk to him.

My father came into the store and asked the lady to follow him out of the store, through the shipping room, and into the kitchen. The kitchen was where my father took care of business. He met with salesmen there. It was where he arranged to buy flour and all of the other things he needed for the bakery. But this time, I thought something bad was happening. I waited a minute and then followed my father and the lady who was still tightly squeezing the bag in her hand. I stood in the back of the kitchen and watched.

My father sat on one side of the kitchen table and the lady on the other side. I could barely hear her. She told my father that she had bought some raisin buns the day before. When she was eating one of them, she saw something in the bun. It wasn't a raisin. It was a fly. Just thinking that she might have eaten the fly made her feel like throwing up. She has felt sick to her stomach every since. She saved the bun with the fly in it. It was in the bag she was holding.

She was going to go to her doctor. She would have to pay for that. Her husband told her that they should sue the bakery. I didn't know what that meant. But I could tell that she wanted my father to give her some money. She told her husband she was sure that Ike Silber would take care of her. That was why she came to the bakery to talk to him.

My father waited. Then he spoke: "Vould you mind? Maybe I could have a look. The bun. A kvik look." The lady slowly let get of the bag. She carefully reached inside and pulled out the remains of the bun in question. She unfolded the waxed paper from around the bun. I could see the tooth marks indented in the bun. It was hard to see anything else about the bun from where I was standing. The lady pointed to something in the bun and said it was the fly. My father leaned over and looked. His face was closer and closer to the bun.

Suddenly, in a split second, my father plucked something from the bun and popped it into his mouth. The lady sucked in her breath. Then she began yelling and screaming. That was the fly. My husband told me you would do something like that.

He told me to be careful. I shouldn't have
let you see the bun. I don't know what I can
tell my husband. You swallowed the fly!

My father stayed very calm. That was very
unusual for him. The lady got more and
more upset. She wouldn't stop crying. My
father told her not to worry. "You vouldn't
be sick anymore. You don haff to go to see
a doctor." It didn't help. She carefully
folded the wax paper around the bun and
put it back in the bag while tears were
running down her face. Still clutching her
treasured bag, the lady headed to the door
leading out of the kitchen. She kept
repeating over and over. You swallowed
the fly. You swallowed the fly. I can't
believe it. You swallowed the fly.

My father stretched his arms in front of
him with his hands pointed upward as if he
was pleading with the lady to understand.
As she opened the door to leave, he tried
once more to console her.

`

"Lady, listen. It vasn't a fly! It vas a raisin in the bun."

13

OUR BABYSITTER

By the time I was nine or ten, my sister Evelyn and I would sometimes be left alone in the house. Not quite alone. We had a babysitter. We were not frightened of being alone. We were terrified of the babysitter.

Our babysitter was the night watchman. I suppose the principal reason my parents hired him was to make sure that no one broke into the bakery. Since our home and the bakery were inexorably connected, the night watchman also did double-duty as our babysitter. His name was Max. It was pronounced "Maachs." Saying his name still makes me shiver. He was creepy.

Max was tall, skinny, and had a cadaverous face. His eyes were sunken, his cheeks bony and strongly prominent under his thin wrinkled skin. Just to look at his grizzly gray stubble of a beard made me feel itchy. Long strands of dirty, matted gray hair cascaded down his back. His neck was elongated, its muscles outlined with craggy folds of skin and his Adam's apple jutted forward like the beak of a bird. He was clothed mostly with a broad, soiled apron wrapped several times around his scrawny body. Under the apron, he wore a grubby work shirt and wrinkled pants, speckled with flour. He wore oversized shoes, more like boots, that were often untied and caked in a paste of flour and sawdust. He was bent over as he walked and his heavy shoes clumped slowly and ominously as he stalked through the bakery.

We only caught glimpses of Max when he first arrived. He spent most of the night in the cellar. He wandered through the stacks of flour stored in the basement, drinking beer as he went along, and he gradually lost himself in unintelligible muttering. The muttering eventually changed to a thin, whispering, reed-like whine. Gradually, his wailing began to take shape as a song with strange German words that we could not understand. Max's singing intensified and pretty soon, his voice rose like the dead in a pathetic lament. As he drank more and more, his voice sounded as if he were howling; gradually his singing deteriorated into awful, pathetic, ghostly, beseeching, frightening, and bloodcurdling moans of agony. At that point, I knew he was completely drunk.

When Max's voice reached its maximum volume it was, of course, impossible to sleep. Evelyn would call out to me and I would dash into her room to comfort her. I could hardly wait for her call, so I would not be alone. I was her older brother and I was not supposed to be afraid. I did not want to go back to my own empty room, so I was glad I had a reason to stay with her. Of course, I needed comforting as much as

`

she. I pretended to her and to myself that there was nothing to be afraid of.

Nothing to be afraid of? But what if Max should decide to come up the cellar stairs slowly, one heavy step at a time, stagger through the bakery, plod into the kitchen, pull open a drawer, grab a knife, thump through the living room, climb, step by step, to the second floor, kick open the bedroom door, and—I tried to stop imagining what would happen next. By now, his singing had begun to diminish in intensity and all that we still heard were occasional bursts of tearful sounds. There were longer periods of silence. Time moved at an agonizingly slow pace. We waited.

Eventually, Max passed out and his terrible, petrifying, menacing lullaby came to an end. Finally, our babysitter was rendered harmless. At last we could go to sleep and feel safe. There was nothing to be afraid of.

`

14

THE MUMMY'S HAND

Saturday was a day of observance. Not of religion but of the movies. My favorite temple was the Fulton Theatre, only a few blocks from home. The first stop was into the bakery where my mother worked behind the counter. I asked for money for the movies, she pressed the "No Sale" key on the cash register, a bell rang, and the drawer opened. She retrieved three nickels and gave them to me. I was on my way. A short trip down Monroe Street, a left turn on Pressman to Fulton Avenue, and I was there.

I used two nickels to buy a ticket and held onto the third for candy. No popcorn, just candy. The purchase was irrevocable and required much thought. The choices included licorice sticks, Good & Plenty, Hershey's Chocolate Bars, Milky Ways,

`

Raisinettes, Peanut Chews, Nonpareils, and Jujubes. Peanut Chews were my favorite. Candy in hand, I settled into a seat. I promised myself that I would not begin eating any candy until the movie began; otherwise, I would run out of candy too soon, not a good way to get through an afternoon of movie watching.

Usually, the show didn't begin exactly at the scheduled time. When that happened, one or two kids began stamping their feet. Then others joined in and pretty soon, the whole theatre was vibrating with the marching rhythm of impatient children. When the first images appeared on screen loud cheers, whistles, and shouts of general jubilation accompanied it. "Previews of Coming Attractions" were the lure to guarantee a full house the following week. This was followed by "Short Subjects," the first of which was one of the "Our Gang" series. A familiar plot involved the gang deciding to put on a show, not having a suitable venue, discovering an abandoned barn, fixing it up, rehearsing, and finally everyone in the neighborhood streaming in for a rousing performance.

"Movietone News" was next. This informed us in a very upbeat way about the state of affairs in the world, no matter how grim the reality. A firm, familiar voice intoned the events of the day in a very authoritative manner. Another favorite was the travelogue. We were taken to an obscure South Sea Island, with swaying palm trees, happy natives beating on coconut shells, passionate tribal dancing, and fishermen in bark canoes paddling furiously out into the ocean. Finally, it ended with the sun sinking into the sea as the announcer in mellifluous voice chanted "...and as the sun slowly sets over the romantic island of Bali Bali, we bid farewell to a land of contentment, hoping that some day we will find our way back to these enchanted shores."

`

We saw the next chapter of one of the Saturday afternoon serials. At the end of the previous week's episode, Buck Rogers was strapped to a table and about to be pulverized with a deadly ray machine operated by a vicious villain on a planet in outer space. The bad guy had just reached for the switch to direct a lethal dose to our hero. How could Buck Rogers possibly survive? Not to worry. At the beginning of the next chapter, a trap door opened beneath the enemy and sent him flying into space. Another implausible episode followed, ending in an equally impossible life-threatening situation for Buck Rogers. To be continued next week.

Finally, the first feature began. It might have been called *Tarzan and the Elephant Burial Ground*. Johnny Weismuller, an Olympic swimmer turned actor, played Tarzan, and there were many scenes of his swimming across lagoons, usually to rescue Jane. In this episode, Tarzan learned that some wicked men were robbing the sacred elephant burial grounds of valuable ivory tusks. A lovable chimpanzee had chattered the news of this terrible misdeed to Tarzan, who understood monkey language. Tarzan swung through the trees on long vines, yodeling his famous cry. All the elephants got the message and came running; Tarzan mounted one of them and led them to the Hidden Burial Grounds. A stampede followed. The greedy hunters were trampled to death. The chimpanzee jumped up and down. Tarzan and Jane were very happy. Me, Tarzan. You, Jane.

The afternoon finale was the second feature, *The Mummy's Hand.* Somewhere in Egypt a group of bad men dressed in jodhpurs and wearing pith helmets were digging into the graves of buried Egyptian pharaohs to steal hidden treasures. As the movie progressed, there was an unexpected slowing of the action, the actors' voices descended into a deep bass, while small black circles expanded on the screen. The film had gotten stuck. Finally the screen went blank. Once again, the stamping began. This time, it was more insistent and accompanied by even louder whistles and shouting. The lights went up. We all turned to the booth behind us to direct our booing to the poor projectionist, struggling to restart the movie. Eventually, the movie resumed; we returned to Egypt and settled back in our seats.

The villains sat at a table trying to decipher an ancient map to find the exact place where gold amulets were hidden. Behind them was a case containing a very old and dusty mummy. Slowly, the mummy began to stir. To our horror, the mummy began to move. The men were not aware of what was going on. The mummy took one step forward, then another. The ribbons of cloth dropped away from the mummy's face to reveal Boris Karloff, looking gaunt, skeletal, and terrifying. The mummy's hand slowly stretched forward. Boris Karloff placed it squarely on the table in front of the bad guys. One of the men saw the hand, realized that the mummy had come to life, and went insane. He screamed. That did it! I was beyond terror. I froze. I remember little of what happened next, but only that I could not leave the theatre. Many people left. The hours passed. I was afraid to move.

A flashlight shone in my eyes. An usher was accompanying my mother down the aisle. She had come to find me. It was late. I told her what had happened. It was the mummy's hand. She was not angry. She understood. I reached for my mother. She took my hand in hers. We left the movies together and headed home.

15

TWO CENTS FOR CANDY

My school was only a few blocks from home. Every day, I returned home for lunch. When lunch was over my mother gave me two cents that I could use to buy candy. I carried the two cents very carefully in one hand, my fists rolled over them very tightly so I would not drop them on my way to school.

There was a candy store across the street from our school. It was very busy right after lunch before the afternoon school session was to begin. Children were packed in the store, waiting their turn to get up to the counter where the candy was displayed in a big glass case. When I could get near the counter, I looked over everything in the case before making a very important decision: how to spend my two cents.

`

One possibility was to buy a coddie for two cents. A coddie was not candy but a fish cake, made of ground- up fish and served on a saltine cracker. It was very delicious, especially when you put a little bit of mustard on top of it. But, if you bought a coddie, that used up all of your money and you didn't have any money left over to buy something else. I only bought a coddie once in a while because I really liked candy even better.

It was hard to choose. I had some favorites. Sometimes, I would get "Dots." They were dots of candy that were stuck on paper. For one cent, the candy lady would tear off a piece that had about six dots on it. That was a good choice because you got a lot for just one cent.

Another good candy was a little wax bottle that looked like a Coca-Cola bottle. You bit off the end of the bottle and sucked the juice out of it. The juice was very sweet and

`

came in different flavors. I bought one of these almost every day. They only cost one cent.

There were round candies that were named Jawbusters because they were so hard. They were not easy to bite into and could really break your jaw if you bit down on them with too much force. I heard that a boy had to go to the hospital when he bit into a Jawbuster that broke his jaw. I was scared this could happen to me; so I just sucked on my Jawbuster and let it melt slowly. That way I wouldn't have to go to the hospital.

Another special candy was a pie that came in a little metal pie tin. The filling had different flavors and tasted just like sugar. The pie came with a little spoon you could use to get the candy out. Nothing tasted sweeter than that.

Sometimes I couldn't make up my mind. I would have to decide in a hurry, because the other children started pushing against me and yelled at me for taking so long. When I was taking too much time, I always had a candy that never failed me. I would choose a licorice stick. It came in two flavors: licorice, which was black, or raspberry, in red. I liked raspberry better.

I would hold onto my candies and push through the crowd of children waiting their turn at the counter. I waited until I was out of the store and on my way to school before I began eating my candy. I wanted the taste of the candy to last as long as it could before school started again. After I crossed the street, I began eating my candy. When I came to the front door of the school, I always finished the last piece of candy before I went inside.

16

SKIPPING

Why was I so nervous? I walked faster and faster through the narrow cobblestoned streets. My wife, Carol, and I were in San Miguel de Allende, a charming haven in Mexico for American travelers. I enrolled in the *Instituto Allende* to take classes in painting and sculpture and to study Spanish. Carol was going to be angry. I was late for lunch. I was short of breath but pushed myself to move more quickly. I began to run and then skip. Skipping and running so I could get to our house in a hurry. Then it began to come together. Skipping.

I was late because my Spanish teacher had asked me to stay after class. Why would she ask me to do that? Had I done something wrong? Was there a problem? She was very reassuring: No, to the contrary. She felt I had caught onto learning Spanish very quickly. She felt I was ahead of everyone in the class and that I should probably join the next level when I returned to the school on the following day. I could skip the rest of the work in the beginning class. I was to skip a year. Skipping. Thinking of skipping brought back a memory. I understood why I was nervous.

Miss Ellison was my second grade teacher. I loved her. She was very kind and had a soft voice. One day she told us how to make butter. She had a small bottle of cream that she poured into a container with a big wooden handle. It was called a churn and you made butter by turning the handle around and around so it mixed up the cream and turned it into butter. We all took turns turning the handle and when we were finished, it worked. Magic. The cream had turned into butter! Miss Ellison put a little bit of butter on crackers and everybody got one of them. It was the most delicious butter I have ever tasted. Sweet and smooth. Sweet like Miss Ellison.

One day Miss Ellison asked me to stay after the morning class was over. Had I done something wrong? Was I in trouble? No, she told me. I was doing very good work in the second grade. Her voice was soft and kind. I was relieved. Then she told me that I was going into the third grade and didn't have to wait until the end of the year. It was called skipping a grade. When I came back from lunch I could start in the third grade with a new teacher. I was very sad that Miss Ellison would not be my teacher but very glad that I hadn't done anything wrong. I looked at the big clock on the wall. I knew I was late for lunch and had to hurry.

All of the other children were far ahead of me and I ran to catch up. I went as fast as I could. I was worried that I was late. I was afraid my mother would be upset with me. I was always on time. I began to run and

`

skip to hurry up. Skipping as fast as I could to get home. I had to wait before I could cross Monroe Street. It was a main street through Baltimore and there were lots of cars. Waiting made me more nervous. Finally, when there was a space between the cars, I ran across the street. I flew up the stairs of our porch and burst into the house.

My mother was in the kitchen waiting for me. What a relief. She did not look angry. She only asked me why I was late. I told her that Miss Ellison kept me after class. Why? Had you done something wrong? No, I explained to my mother, I was going to skip. Skip? Yes, it was called skipping. I was going to skip the rest of the second grade. When I went back to school for the afternoon, I was going into the third grade. My mother said that was very nice. I had lunch and when I went back to school, I said goodbye to Miss Ellison and went into the third grade. There were no conferences

`

with parents, no special tests, none of that. You just skipped.

When I remembered all of this, I calmed down. Carol was very happy to see me. She noticed that I was a little later than usual and asked why. I explained about what had happened. I was going to go into the next year of Spanish. It was called skipping. She thought that was great and gave me a big hug.

`

17

DON'T MENTION IT

Nobody said anything about it. My classmate, Billy, had been absent for more than two weeks. Our third grade teacher never said a word. Where was Billy? I wondered about what had happened to him. Finally, at recess, one of my friends, Marvin, told me.

Did you hear about Billy? What about Billy? He died. He died? Yeah, he died. What from? He went to the hospital. They did an operation. He had to have his tonsils out. They gave him too much gas. He died. He died? Yeah, he died. Wanna see his body? Whaddya mean? They're going to have a funeral but first they have his body in a coffin. Yeah? Yeah. We can go see him. Where? In his house. You sure? Yeah, I'm sure. Is it OK? Sure, it's OK. Are you going?

`

Yeah. Wanna come? Is it OK? Sure. I'll meet you after school and we'll go together.

I was scared but I couldn't back out. I wasn't sure it was all right to see a dead body, especially because we were Jewish. I thought we shouldn't do it and that there was something wrong about it. I hoped Marvin would forget about it but he was waiting for me after school just as he had said. We set off together and headed up Baker Street to Billy's house. As we got closer to his house, I walked more and more slowly. Marvin was impatient with me. C'mon. Don't take all day.

We climbed the steps leading to Billy's house. I thought we should turn around and go back. But, before I could say anything, Marvin rang the doorbell. Billy's mother opened the door. She asked us to come in. I didn't know what you were supposed to say but I mumbled something. She thanked us for coming and pointed to the dining room.

I began to feel cold drops of sweat trickling down my forehead. I felt there was ice in my stomach and I thought I might throw up. The room seemed to get very dark when I looked inside. On the table there was a coffin. It was like a new, polished piece of furniture, shiny and dark. I tried not to look, but I couldn't stop looking at the same time. I glanced sideways at first so I wouldn't see. But then, I did see.

It was Billy, but it wasn't exactly Billy. His eyes were closed but somehow he didn't look like he was asleep. His face was shiny as though it was coated with wax. His lips were too red, and so were his cheeks. His hair, neatly parted to one side, glistened and looked as though it had been plastered down. He was wearing a white shirt and a blue tie. He never dressed like that at school. I looked at Billy for only a split second and turned away as fast as I could. I was afraid to look at him but the picture of him in the coffin wouldn't go away. I

126

`

started to shiver and had to get out in a hurry. I was afraid I would pee.

We didn't stay much longer. More people were coming in the house and we said goodbye to Billy's mother. When we got outside, I wanted to go home as fast as I could. I felt we had done something wrong. I don't know how I knew this, but I told Marvin that because we were Jewish, we had to wash our hands. He didn't believe me at first. Wash our hands? Yeah. Why? I don't know why but I think we're supposed to wash our hands. How are we going to wash our hands? Look, there's a spigot over there.

A few houses away, a garden hose was coiled up next to an outside faucet. We looked to make sure no one saw us. Each of us took turns opening the tap and running water over our hands. It somehow made me feel I had done something to make up for seeing Billy dead. I had never seen a dead person before. I kept seeing Billy's face, shiny and covered with wax, looking like Billy, but not being Billy.

Marvin and I walked together without saying anything. I said goodbye to him when we got to his house on Appleton Street. Then I turned on Westwood Avenue and walked toward our house on Monroe Street. I went inside. I was glad no one paid any attention to my coming home late from school. I needed to be by myself. I never mentioned to anyone that Billy had died and that I had seen his body. I was glad I had washed my hands afterwards.

18

PROTECTION MONEY

McKean Avenue was a dangerous place for Jewish boys. I never set foot on McKean Avenue. Bad Irish Catholic boys lived there. Jews lived a block away on Monroe Street and the boundary was very clear. If you were a sensible Jewish boy, you avoided McKean Avenue to ensure your survival into adulthood.

Not all of the McKean Avenue boys went to Catholic School. Some attended P.S. 29, the neighborhood elementary school. Part of the art of self-protection was to become invisible to McKean Avenue boys. I took pride in learning to identify them. I figured out ways to stay away from them, to find other parts of the playground distant from them and to never stand near them in line. They never laid a finger on me. I was really smart. I heard stories about other Jewish boys being beaten up. Not me. That never happened.

Fortunately, I was sent to a special junior high school that was not in our neighborhood, so I never had to contend with McKean Avenue boys at school again. When at home in the neighborhood, I kept my distance from them so I grew up unscathed. That doesn't mean they didn't have a grip on me. I was terrified of them. For years, just the words, *McKean Avenue*, struck fear in my heart.

Many years later, I was invited to attend a reunion of alumni of P.S. 29. What a great treat! It was a chance to meet neighborhood and childhood friends. But, what if some of the McKean Avenue boys— now men—would be there? I could just talk to them, I told myself. Nothing to be afraid of now. Should I play it safe and stay away? Of course not. Face it like a man. So, I went.

`

The reunion was like many others. Most of the people did not look like anyone I had known as a child. How had everyone grown so old? There were a few that I recognized. Slowly, I would form an image of one of the adults as a child and recollections of playing together floated to the surface. We remembered our most beloved teachers: Miss Ellison and Mrs. Smith. We recalled the games we played together at recess, especially "Crack the Whip," one of my favorites. But suddenly, there they were: I spotted some of the McKean Avenue boys.

I had recalled them as giants, but, to my amazement, they had shrunk. They were now about the same height as I was. Gathering my courage, I walked toward them. Nothing to be afraid of, I kept repeating to myself. Just say "hello." I did. No one hit me. I decided to speak to them. I was brave enough to tell them how scared of them I had been when we were at school together. We began to tell stories about growing up in the neighborhood. I learned things from them I had never known before.

During the Depression, their priest at the neighborhood church praised my father. When there was little food for many families, my father gave away unsold bread to anyone who came to the bakery looking for food. My father had helped his neighbors, including those who lived on McKean Avenue, to survive the hard times. They were grateful to him. Yet knowing this about my father didn't lessen their hatred of Jews in general. Any Jew that wandered onto McKean Avenue was fair game.

Then came the most astonishing revelation of all: "Do you know why we never beat you up?" one of the men asked me. "No," I said, "Why?" "Your mother paid us five cents a week to make sure we would never hit you," he told me.

`

At first, I couldn't be sure I had heard them. I held back tears. I could never have dreamed or imagined what they told me. My mother had paid protection money? How innocent I had been. How naïve in believing that I had been so clever in avoiding my persecutors. Now they had given me a precious gift: the knowledge that it was my mother who was my protector. I had never known. I wanted to talk to her and to thank her.

When I next visited my mother in the nursing home, she could neither remember the past nor know who I was. Sadly, I realized that I would never be able to let her know how grateful I was. I said goodbye to her and headed for my car. When I began to drive and was alone, the dam broke. I sobbed. Tears flooded my cheeks. I had to stop driving. I couldn't see in front of me, but my vision of my past had been changed forever. I wanted my mother back, if only for a moment to thank her. It was too late.

19

THE ICEMAN COMETH

The ice truck pulled up in front of our house. Lefty, the iceman, got out and quickly surveyed the windows of the houses before beginning his deliveries. Cards, displayed in the windows of each home, told him what size ice was needed. On the four sides of the card were printed: *5, 10, 25, or 50 cents.* The cards were turned so that the number at the top was the amount of ice Lefty was to deliver that day. Lefty walked to the back of the truck and pulled aside a tarpaulin to reveal his precious cargo of massive blocks of ice. Like a skilled gymnast, he vaulted up on the truck. Then, with a precision equaled only by an Italian stonecutter, he began the process of carving out sections of ice. He carried a short axe, his surgical scalpel.

`

Lefty lifted his axe, swung it overhead in a wide arc and, with uncanny accuracy, planted the blade in the ice. With repeated blows of the axe, he split the ice into two pieces of identical size. Then, with the same exactness, he created smaller blocks of ice in precise subdivisions. Meanwhile, slivers of ice of various sizes flew from his axe, collateral damage resulting from his surgical strikes. Lefty hopped down from the truck, reached for a pair of huge tongs, opened their jaws and grabbed hold of a piece of ice. He covered his shoulder with a swath of burlap and in one quick motion, hoisted the ice onto his back, holding fast to the tongs. This was the moment we had been waiting for.

We knew that Lefty would now deliver the ice to one of the houses. There were no refrigerators, but iceboxes. These were made of wood, the upper section the repository for the ice and the bottom for perishable food. In a few minutes, Lefty would be opening the ice section and depositing his cargo before heading back to the truck to make his next delivery. We moved like sleek jungle cats stalking their prey. Our target: the deliciously cold slivers of ice. They were the popsicles of our time. They were free. They offered a moment of respite on a scorching summer day. They were even more delicious because they were "stolen" from the ice truck. They were connected with the exhilarating excitement of escaping the danger of getting caught.

We grabbed slivers of ice and ran, our hearts pounding. We were on our way darting around the corner from Monroe Street on to Westwood Avenue when Lefty would emerge from a delivery. He ran after us, flailing his arms and shouting in mock rage that we were to keep away from his truck. He never caught us. I had not realized then that he understood precisely his part in this game. It would have spoiled everything for us to have been *caught.* Everything would have become serious

`

then. The joke would be over. The fun would be gone. The heat of the Baltimore summer would have become unbearable.

20

TO THE BEACH

One summer morning I woke up early. We were going to the beach! There was much hustle and bustle in the house. I got dressed quickly and ran downstairs, afraid

`

I might be left behind. My father was already loading our car, the Reo. He stacked some of the suitcases on the running board—a long, narrow platform that helped you to step into the car. He tied the rest of the luggage to the back of the car. After all the bags were arranged, he pulled an accordion-like fence across the running board side of the car to keep all the suitcases from falling off. We got in the car from the other side.

I remember our trip to the beach the first summer after Evelyn was born. She was an infant, all of five months old. There was a hammock connected with hooks to the ceiling of the car, behind the front seat. My mother bundled Evelyn up in blankets and placed her in the hammock. Libbye, Myer, and I sat in the back. My mother settled in the front seat. My father assumed his customary position in the driver's seat. We took off.

`

It was a long drive. There were no superhighways, mostly two, sometimes three-lane roads, so the going was slow. I looked forward to our arrival at the ferry to cross the Chesapeake Bay. We usually had to wait behind a long line of cars until we finally got the signal to go ahead. The car made lots of noise when it crossed the threshold onto the ferryboat. We got out of the car and could walk around the boat. I liked to go to the front, watch the waves and pretend we were crossing the ocean. The final leg of the car trip seemed endless. I watched the billboards to pass the time. I loved the Burma Shave jingles, one, especially: *He played...Sax...Had no B.O....But his Whiskers Scratched... So she let him go...Burma Shave.* At long last, we arrived in Wildwood, New Jersey, where we were to spend five or six weeks.

My parents never arranged for a house in advance. Instead, we drove all around Wildwood, looking for a place. When we saw a "For Rent" sign, we would stop and

`

my mother would get out to look over the accommodations. After surveying three or four houses, she and my father would decide which one we would rent. It was a great relief to unpack and settle in. The houses seemed large. I remember one that was my favorite; it had snowball plants in front, just like those in front of my grandmother Bubbe's house in Baltimore. That made it seem familiar and safe.

There was usually a long walk to the beach. It was exciting to arrive at the boardwalk, climb the stairs, and catch a first glimpse of the ocean. We ran down to the beach, staked out our territory with towels and umbrellas, then without a moment's hesitation, ran lickety-split across the sand, into the water, up to our knees, splashing against the surf, finally flinging ourselves into one of the waves. There were usually sandbars not far from the shoreline to swim to, where we could stand protected from the force of the waves. We lost track of time catching waves to body surf. We spent endless hours digging in the sand and building castles, villages, waterways for moats, and gathering shells to decorate our elaborate structures.

In the evening, we walked along the boardwalk. We bought ice cream on a stick, dipped in chocolate like Good Humor bars, only these were made right in front of your eyes. They tasted even better than the ones we bought from a truck. Along the boardwalk, we sometimes would go into a Fun House. There were long slides from the second floor, huge, rotating barrel wheels to walk through without losing your balance, a huge flat disc on which you sat securely as it began rotating slowly at first, picking up speed, then spinning so fast that you were flung out like a shooting star. Further down the boardwalk was one of my favorite spots, The Flea Circus.

When Evelyn was older, she and I would stand together, transfixed as we watched fleas perform miraculous feats. They were dressed as cowboys, with chaps, and sometimes hauled little wagons. No one believed we had seen this actually happen, but we were certain that our eyes had not deceived us.

Sometimes, my sister Libbye and I got aboard little cars that took us through The Haunted House. It was scary. Skeletons popped out. Spider webs brushed across our face. Windows flew open and skulls appeared. The car jerked about, then plunged into totally pitch-black space. A blood-curdling shriek would suddenly penetrate the darkness. We screamed, clung to each other, and said it was fun even though we could hardly wait for the car to arrive at the last door, break through it, and deposit us suddenly outside, into the light.

When we were older, we did not rent a house. Instead, we stayed in style at a first-class hotel near the end of the boardwalk: Musher's Hotel. It was enormous. It must have had at least eight or nine stories.

`

After we returned from the beach, we entered the hotel from the basement, where there were showers and places to dry off and change before going up to our rooms. In the bathroom, the tub had a special faucet in case you wanted to take a salt-water bath. But the best thing about the hotel was the meals.

A boy would go through the hotel lobby playing perfect arpeggios on an instrument like a little xylophone to announce supper. People waited for that signal and then poured into the dining room. The meals could have fed entire cities. There were many choices, many courses, many dishes, many vegetables, and many desserts. There was hardly enough room on each table to accommodate all of the china necessary to contain enough food to satisfy the insatiable appetites of robust, overweight Jewish families.

There was no sunscreen in those days. I had bright red hair and a complexion to match. Sun was not my friend. My mother dressed me in long shirts and pants at the beach to protect me. It was no use. After the first few days, I was red. My mother tried many remedies to relieve the pain. We bought Noxzema by the carload and slathered it on my fiery skin. But I especially remember one of the home remedies. My mother had heard that egg white was the treatment of choice. I would be coated with it. It dried into a thin shell and I felt encased in a straight jacket. I believe it actually helped by forming a coating of protein that somehow was a little soothing, but it was mostly my mother's ministrations and caring that gave me some sense of relief and hope that the burning would go away.

The days at the beach seemed to stretch endlessly as the summer wore on. We were joined in some years by my sister Rosalie and my brothers Sam and Bernard. In addition, we often connected with my Aunt Mitzi, Aunt Katie, Uncle Jack, and my

`

cousins Leonard and Elsie. Elsie always seemed to be unhappy. It seemed that something was always making her cry. I could never understand why, and I never found out. Leonard and I played together and built elaborate structures in the sand.

One year, we dug a big hole in the sand large enough for us to sit in. We stuck a shovel in the sand in front of the hole and pretended we were driving a car by turning the shovel and making a noise like a car—varroom! varroom! We were in the driver's seat; we were in charge; we were in control. My Uncle Jack tried to take over our game and insisted on getting into our "car." He was too big. The walls crumbled and he destroyed our magnificent creation. I was very angry. There was nothing Leonard and I could do. He had not only burst the walls of our construction, but had also burst into our make-believe world.

I always believed that if there were only no adults around, we could have managed perfectly by ourselves and lived on happily forever building castles in the sand. My dream was that the summer would never end. But it did. We had to pack up and leave. Everything had to be fitted again into the car. When we were ready to leave, I reluctantly took my place in the car. I slouched in the back seat. I hardly remember the car trip from Wildwood back to Baltimore. I slept most of the way.

21

A REAL MAGICIAN

It was not a sunny day. There were grey clouds in the sky. It looked like it was going to rain. Not a day to go to the beach. After breakfast, I asked my cousin Leonard if he wanted to go to the boardwalk with me. He thought that was a good idea and we set out together.

From the boardwalk, we could see the ocean. There were big waves and nobody was swimming. Red flags were planted in the sand. That meant that you were not supposed to go in the water. The air felt wet, almost like it was going to start raining any minute.

We walked toward an old movie theatre but there wasn't going to be a movie. The sign said there was a magic show. It was about to start. We wanted to keep warm so we decided we would go to the show. It was a good thing I had a quarter in my pocket. That was enough to pay for our tickets and I had enough left over to buy some candy.

Most of the seats were taken, but some in the front row were empty. We sat down and waited for the show to begin. Up on the stage, there was a big velvet curtain that opened and a man dressed in a black suit, even a black shirt, came out. He was wearing a top hat. He was the magician. "Ladies and gentlemen," he said. "The magic show is about to begin. But first I need a volunteer to help me with my magic tricks. Who would like to volunteer?"

I don't know why, but my arm shot up in the air just like lightning, all by itself. I shouted along with the other kids, "Me! Me! Me!" Much to my amazement, the magician pointed to me and said, "You with the red hair. Come up on the stage and help me with my magic tricks."

I couldn't believe that I had been chosen. But I had. So I left my seat, walked along the front of the stage to the stairs at the side, and began climbing up step by step to become the magician's helper. I was excited and afraid at the same time. It all happened so fast that it seemed like everything was going on without my really deciding to do it.

I stood by the magician. He leaned down and shook my hand. He asked me if I would like to help him with his magic tricks. I said yes. Then he asked me my name. "Earle," I said. He turned to the audience. "Earle is going to be my helper." Then he turned to me and said something that changed my life. It was then that I knew that he was a real magician.

"Earle is an English name," he said. "You must be English. You must come from a noble English family if you are an earl."

What magic! Everything changed. The coldness of the day changed. The sun was shining inside. I felt very warm all over. I wondered how the magician knew something that even I didn't know but had suspected for a long time: I was in the wrong family. I didn't know it for sure until he said what he said. He made everything clear. All the years I had lived with four brothers and three sisters was a mistake. My father and mother were not my true parents. Somehow, there had been a big mix-up. I actually was from a noble English family. And, besides, why would I have been named Earle? What kind of name is Earle for a Jewish boy like me?

I don't remember all of the magic he performed after that. But I know that he pulled money from my ears and had me examine boxes to make sure they were empty. Then rabbits appeared. Birds flew out of his top hat. A lady was sawed in half but she was still alive. A white scarf changed into a streamer of rainbow colors.

`

Flames shot out of nowhere. I was in a daze.

None of that magic was as great as his knowing the magic of my name and the magic of a long-lost secret that only he knew about. How did he know? How could he tell? I really came from another family. I was an English earl. That was the real magic, and I was sure that he was a real magician.

`

22

HOT POTATO

By the time I was ten, I did not need a Boy Scout manual to learn how to build a fire. As controlled as I was inside our house during the day, the opposite was often true at night. Child rearing in our family paradoxically combined tyrannical discipline with unsupervised neglect; so, after dinner, it was very easy to slip out of the house, unnoticed, to meet up with my friends. One night I got together with Herbie Adler (a friend), Leonard Sollins (my cousin), and Leonard Mogul (who lived upstairs in my cousin's house).

Why not get some potatoes so we could roast them in a fire? Great idea. But we had to have a plan. This took some preparation. We'd have to wait until the next night to carry this off. We promised that each of us would steal a potato from home. I pledged

`

that I would find some matches with which to start a fire. If all went according to plan, we were to meet at the railroad yard the next evening. Why did we decide to meet there?

At the foot of Appleton Street, there were spur railroad tracks where unused cars were stored, waiting to be returned to service. We often played around these abandoned cars and had already discovered that on the outside of the train wheels, there were little boxes that contained wool-like material loaded with grease to lubricate the wheels. Wouldn't this stuff be perfect for starting a fire? The boxes were hinged, so it would be easy to reach into them and retrieve the ready-made kindling

The following day, I found a time to wander into the kitchen without being noticed and to surreptitiously remove a potato from its bin and slip it into my pocket. Still unseen, I quickly grabbed a bunch of matches from a box and stuffed them alongside my stolen potato. I casually sauntered out of the kitchen. My heart pounded against my chest. I had carried off the heist safely. No one had seen me. There was no way I would be caught. The rest of the day seemed to stretch out forever. I could hardly wait for nightfall, when we would execute our daring plan.

Finally, dinner was over. I moved slowly across the living room and glided out the front door. I took a few steps to the corner and then, scarcely taking note of the break in traffic, ran across Monroe Street. Mrs. Rhody, as usual, was positioned like a policeman on duty in front of her house and screamed at me, "One day you'll get killed if you ever run into traffic like that again." I ran even faster, just to get away from her screeching voice. I slowed down to catch my breath and walked past Sherman's grocery store, continued one block along Westwood Avenue and turned left on Appleton Street to our designated meeting place. We gathered at the railroad yard.

Each of us had brought a potato. I had the matches. We foraged in the dark and found scraps of wood that we gathered together in a very haphazard pile. Finally, the last crucial step in preparing the fire: retrieving the kindling from the train wheels. Herbie lifted the lid near one of the wheels, and I reached inside to pull out a handful of greasy fur. Adding this to the pile completed the preparation. Each of us removed stolen potatoes from our pockets and placed them ceremoniously on the stack. Since I had stolen the matches, I had the distinct honor of lighting the fire. I scratched a match on the cement floor of the railroad yard and touched it to the pyre.

Immediately, wonderful flames shot up and we all jumped back. How glorious! Our faces were lit up not only by the fire, but also by the excitement of doing something

`

so unmistakably bad and dangerous. We
moved closer together and warmed
ourselves around the fire while our
potatoes blackened. With a few long sticks,
we retrieved our potatoes, gingerly picked
them up and tossed them from one hand to
hand to avoid being burned. When they
had cooled sufficiently, we peeled away the
charred crust and reached into the
charcoaled mass to mash together in our
fingers whatever was left of the hot,
delicious, purloined, steamy, crumbly hot
potatoes.

We did not wait for the fire to die out of its
own accord. There was one final ritual to
perform. The fire had to be extinguished.
Each of us unbuttoned his fly and we
displayed to one another our pride and joy.
We all peed together. The fire sizzled and
sputtered, the flames subsided, and clouds
of uriniferous steam and smoke billowed
up and burned our eyes. We didn't know
about bonding in those days. We just knew

`

we were friends forever and that a hot
potato had secured our nascent manhood.

23

MY DAY AT THE CIRCUS

I was playing marbles with Herbie Adler on Appleton Street when the word spread like wildfire: "There's a parade. It's the circus!" We ran like crazy, legs churning, our hearts bursting out of our chests, barely catching our breath, afraid we would be too late. We streaked down Presbury Street to the corner of Fulton Avenue. We made it in time. There it was. A real, live circus parade.

Trainers were seated majestically atop a line of elephants. Each elephant was holding the tail of the one in front of it and they were all decorated with bright red and yellow powder. An especially indelible impression was made by the mammoth, steaming turds that the elephants dropped along the way. They were followed by troops of men armed with shovels and brooms, cleaning up as they marched along, leaving little trace of the elephants' mementos.

Horses in full regalia, plumes of feathers at the tops of their heads, pulled gaudily decorated cages of lions, tigers, and monkeys. Cowboys on horseback, jugglers and prancing acrobats followed. Clowns with big red noses squeezed horns and moved in and out of the crowds. A calliope ended the parade, steaming and puffing, with clanging cymbals marking time to an up-beat march. Herbie and I decided we would meet and go to the circus together that night.

The circus set up tents beyond Easterwood Park. We crossed the park and caught sight of an open lot that had been transformed. In addition to the Big Top, there was a cluster of other, smaller tents with special attractions. We did not have enough money to get in, but Herbie saw other boys crawling under the tent. I was scared. He

`

reassured me. We found a likely spot. He went under the tent first. I thought of running home, but that would be cowardly. I took a final look in both directions to make sure no one was watching, and took a deep breath. The next moment, it was over. I was inside. We clamored to find some empty seats.

It was impossible to follow everything that was going on. It was, in fact, a three-ring circus, with acts being performed in each ring. Trapeze artists sailed overhead, a small car unloaded an unbelievable number of clowns, lions were tamed, people were shot out of canons, dancers pirouetted from one horse to another, elephants stood on hind legs, one against the other, seals played "My Country, 'Tis of Thee" by honking horns. But for me, the climax of the evening took place in one of the smaller tents.

There was a banner overhead announcing Fatima, the Belly Dancer. Would they allow

`

an eleven-year-old boy to get in? How could I miss it? I had the requisite fifteen cents and, standing on my toes to appear taller, placed my money on the counter. No questions asked. I was in. The tent was dimly lit and the floor was covered with tattered oriental rugs. A rope kept the small audience on one side of the tent. We lined up eagerly. A man wearing a funny turban came out and started a phonograph record. Soon the sound of high-pitched, squeaky flute music used to charm snakes, accompanied by a pulsating, persistent drumbeat, filled the air with excitement.

Suddenly, a curtain parted and out came Fatima, shimmying and undulating, with much flesh exposed around her middle. She embraced the pole in the center of the tent, rubbed herself against it as she leaned back, waving her arms frantically. I knew this was really bad and that I shouldn't be there. But that only added to my excitement, which, at that point, was becoming obvious. Fatima came closer and closer to the roped-off area. She was right in front of me, wriggling and gyrating.

I can never be sure, but in the midst of all the frenzy, I thought her hand glanced across a now prominent part of me. But then, the most unkind cut of all. She looked down at me and said in a throaty, accented voice, "Little boy, does your mother know you're here?" and moved away. I was crushed. The excitement vanished. I was deflated. When Fatima disappeared at the back of the tent, I avoided looking at anyone and stepped quickly through the exit. I was sober now. The intoxication was gone. I needed to be home. I was exhausted by my day at the circus.

`

24

A PLACE TO PLAY

Who needed country clubs? We had our parks. Open twenty-four hours a day and free of charge. The parks were our playground and a safe place to play and grow up in. The nearest to our home was Easterwood Park.

There were no leagues, no try-outs for teams. You just showed up at the park and joined a game of softball. There were one or two park people who kept track of equipment, but that was all the adult supervision necessary. All the requisite resources were there: swings, seesaws, sandboxes, tennis courts, and ball fields. I spent endless hours there, not only during the day but also sometimes into the early evenings. A favorite team game was called "Red Line" and involved hiding behind trees and trying to get to home base

`

without being tagged. At the end of the game, we called "Ollie Ollie in Free!" That meant no one could be tagged and we could all come back and declare the game ended.

The bigger and even more magnificent park was Druid Hill Park, slightly farther away from home than Easterwood. It occupied a large swath of northwest Baltimore. A large reservoir formed the southern boundary of the park and the road around the reservoir was closed on Sundays for bike riding. In the summer, we walked around the reservoir to the swimming pool nearby. My first visit to the pool is colored with embarrassment.

I was five and could not go alone. My mother brought me to the pool and I was not allowed to go into the men's locker room by myself. Feeling full of shame, we entered on the women's side. As we undressed, I tried to hide. I cannot distinguish whether I was uncomfortable about being seen, or seeing my mother, each of us at one point naked in front of the other. When I was a few years older I graduated and entered on the men's side where I felt I belonged.

Admission was five cents, which bought you a towel, an elastic wristband with a locker number attached, and a large box in which to place your clothes. Bathing suits for boys were made of itchy wool, all in one piece, with shoulder straps and cut-out circles on the sides. You changed in a cubicle, placed your clothes in the box and gave it to an attendant. I still remember the impression on my feet made by the sisal rugs that led out of the locker room. I would race through the required shower, run down one or two more steps, wade into the pool, and finally throw myself into the water. The pool was huge. A fence separated the deep water, and admission to this part of the pool required swimming a prescribed length without touching the sides.

`

After a long afternoon in the pool, we reluctantly headed back to the locker room. We changed into our clothes and met under a large oak tree just outside the pool. We munched on candy bars as we trod our way home, smelling of chlorine, exhausted, and pleasantly cooled.

The zoo was one of my favorite sections of the park. I felt a special affinity for an elephant named Mary Ann, whose birthday was March 13, 1925, just one day after mine. I visited her religiously whenever we went to the zoo; I bought peanuts and fed them to her. I was very sad when, in later years, I learned that she had died.

One of the small lakes in the park was a favorite place for sailing miniature boats. My brother Sidney made model boats along with a friend whose father ran a hardware store on Westwood and Fulton Avenues. I had fun watching them release their boats into the water. We all cheered when the boats sailed off, propelled by

little engines, just the way they were
intended

Summers in Baltimore were unbearable.
Nights brought no relief from hot, humid
days. There were no air conditioners, only
fans that feebly circulated warm air
ineffectually. To make matters worse, the
radiant heat of the bakery ovens on the
first floor warmed our bedrooms even
more. There was only one solution: head
for Druid Hill Park! On nights that were
especially hot, we gathered up blankets
and pillows and walked to the park. We
trundled up Monroe Street and turned on
Clifton Avenue, where other pilgrims often
joined us, making their way to cooler sites.
On entering the park, people searched in
every direction to find a comfortable spot
to spread their blankets. We looked up at
the stars. We slept soundly. We were not
afraid. It was a real joy; something the
Yiddish word *mechaieh* describes exactly.

In the winter, when the lakes froze, we would ice skate on them. One of the lakes had a small island in its center with a small pagoda-like shelter where we would sometimes build a fire to keep ourselves from freezing. One winter, I skated too close to the edge of the lake where the ice was very thin; it cracked and I descended feet first into the freezing, bone-chilling water. Fortunately, the lake was shallow and I landed, still upright, on the bottom of the lake, thoroughly soaked up to my hips. I quickly pulled myself out, changed into my shoes and raced home. My legs and feet were slowly congealing into blocks of ice. I was frightened that I would be punished. I snuck into the house without being noticed, raced to my room and changed into warm clothes without being seen. I never told anyone what had happened.

As the years passed, and even after we left Monroe Street for a more suburban life, the park remained a playground, albeit of a different sort. This time, it was under cover

`

of dark. The park was a perfect place to drive with dates, pull into a remote spot and, protected by the night, explore the mysterious world of sensual pleasure. It was still a safe place to play and to grow up.

25

MY ALLEYS

The dictionary defines an alley simply as "a narrow back street." Oh no! "My" alleys were much more than that. There were alleys on both sides of Monroe Street, where we lived. Very important things happened in my alleys.

As soon as the weather was warm, wagons began appearing, drawn by horses that looked very tired. They plodded along and pulled their heavy loads behind them. The first to appear was a wagon guided by a black man, who sat on top, slapped a long, thin branch of wood on the horse's back, and called out a song in a loud voice, "Any ole ra-ags...any ole clowe-owes" over and over, keeping time to the clippedy cloppedy sound that the horse made with his hooves on the pavement. Once in a while someone came out of his back door

`

with a bundle and gave it to the ragman. He took hold of the bag, nodded his head, and tossed the rags into his wagon. Then he moved on. "Any ole ra-ags...any ole clowe-owes."

My favorite wagon was the one driven by the watermelon man. That wagon came up the alley only in the hot part of the summer. That was when watermelons were ripe. His wagon was filled with watermelons and his horse had a much heavier load to pull. He sat on top of his wagon like the other man, but he had a much sweeter song to sing. "Wadder melon...Red to da rye-yand." He sang it over and over. "Wadder melon...Red to da rye-yand." Like the ragman's, the beat of the watermelon man's song and the sound of his horse's hooves fit together exactly. If you wanted to buy a watermelon, the watermelon man would give you, for free, a wedge to taste. I never saw anybody who didn't like the taste and didn't buy a watermelon.

`

Then there was another man: the knife-grinder. He wheeled something that looked like a bicycle wheel. Only it was made of stone and it was used for sharpening knives. He did not have a song. He would stop at each house and go through the gate up to the back door. When someone answered, he asked if they wanted him to sharpen their knives. Most of the time, he came away without any knives but once in a while, he would bring some knives with him. I loved to watch him grind the knives. He worked the pedals attached to the wheel, making the wheel go around while he scraped the knives across the wheel to sharpen them. Sometimes sparks would fly. It was very exciting.

Of course, the horses had to "go." They did it as they walked along; leaving clumps of huge turds that fell and stayed on the pavement. There were big puddles of pee, too. It gave the alleys a really bad smell. Sometimes, the ragman and the watermelon man had to make a pee. They got off their wagons and while their horses waited, they peed against a telephone pole.

My friends, Marvin Leventon, Herbie Adler, and I did some really bad things in the alley. When it was near Halloween, there were two special nights. Two nights before Halloween was called "Chalk Night." We got hold of big pieces of chalk and went up and down the alley making big streaks of chalk over all of the garage doors. Then we ran away. The next night was called "Moving Night." That night we did worse things than on Chalk Night. We went around to the back of each house and, wherever we could, we took the gates off fences and hung them up on top of the fence or on a garage. We ran away very fast. I was really scared we would get caught but we never were. So we did it again the next year.

On the other side of Monroe Street, there was another alley that was different. We

`

played games there. There weren't horses and wagons that went up this alley, so it was cleaner and didn't smell bad. We found old rubber heels from abandoned shoes and used them to play hopscotch. To play this game you used chalk to make a design with squares and a round part on the pavement. You threw the rubber heel on one of the spaces in the drawing. Then you had to hop on one foot, bend over, pick up the rubber heel, and hop back to the place where you started.

Sometimes, we jumped rope in the alley. A person on each end of the rope swung the rope around. You had to jump in just at the right time and skip so you didn't get your feet caught in the rope. Some of the girls learned how to jump double-dutch. The rope was doubled over to make it harder to jump. I could never do double-dutch. But I did like regular rope jumping. I still remember the song we used to sing while we jumped rope:

`

Johnny over the ocean, Johnny over the sea.

Johnny broke a milk bottle and blamed it on me.

I told Ma. Ma told Pa. Johnny got a lickin'.

So Ha, Ha, Ha!

One last thing we did in the alley. There was another game we played in secret. It was the "doctor" game. We saved Popsicle sticks. We pretended that we were sick and had to see the doctor. The person who played the doctor took down our pants and had to take our temperature. I am too embarrassed to say where we put the Popsicle sticks.

26

WESTWARD HO!

The day had finally come. I was 11, and I was going to camp. Everything I needed for camp had been labeled and packed in a small trunk and was ready to go. I was excited and a little scared. But mostly, I was happy that I would be getting away from home. I said goodbye to my mother and left through the kitchen into the shipping room of the bakery. Dave Gordon, one of the bakery drivers, was going to take me to the train station.

We drove up Monroe Street to North Avenue and turned left. After a short drive, we arrived at the railroad station near Walbrook Junction. I looked at the sign. It said: *WESTERN MARYLAND RAILWAY.* Gee whiz! I was going out west. It was hard to believe. But there was the sign. There could be no mistake. I would be following

`

in the footsteps of explorers who traveled
across the Great Plains and climbed the
Rocky Mountains. Dave unloaded my trunk
and waited with me until the train arrived.
There were other boys waiting with their
parents and some older boys who were
counselors. We were all headed for Camp
Airy.

Soon I could hear a train far away. The
whistle got higher and higher as the train
approached. The engine noise grew louder.
It made a thundering sound as it came into
sight. The engine was puffing away. Steam
was shooting from the engine. There were
huge wheels turning round and round. The
engine slowed and finally screeched to a
halt. The sound hurt my ears. The engine
was enormous. There was a coal car and
then three or four passenger cars attached.
Dave made sure I joined the rest of the
group. I said goodbye, climbed up the
stairs, and got on board.

`

The inside of the train looked just the way I
had seen trains in movies about the West.
The seats were made of red velvet and
looked worn and a little raggedy. Some of
the windows were half opened. There was
a sharp smell of steam mixed with coal and
there was coal dust over all the window
ledges. We were really going out west. It
was hard to believe. I sat down and waved
goodbye to Dave, who was waiting outside
the train station. Very slowly the train
started to move, jerked, stopped for a
second, and then started up again. It
moved faster and faster and slowly picked
up steam. It huffed and puffed for about
two hours before it began slowing down. I
looked out of the window. There were
mountains in the distance. They must be
the Rocky Mountains.

We stopped at a small road crossing and
everyone scrambled down the steps,
claimed his trunk with the help of the
counselors. The train pulled away, we
crossed the tracks, and walked a short

distance to the camp. I was given blankets and towels and told which bunk I was in. My bunk was a short walk up a hill. After getting settled in our bunk and meeting the other boys, we climbed a very steep hill to get to a big house at the top where we had our meals. Along the way we passed a huge boulder, which further confirmed for me that we were in the West. The other boys told me it was called Piss Rock, for reasons that I learned about later on.

Camp Airy was made for me. The two weeks I spent there were the happiest I can ever remember. I thought that staying for two weeks meant going for the whole season because there were some boys who stayed for only one week. The time flew by. I signed up for everything I could. I did nature studies, lots of swimming, horseback riding (I had to pay for this out of the money I took with me), arts and crafts, volleyball, and had a part in the chorus of "HMS Pinafore." On Friday night, we got in a bus and went to Camp Louise, a

`

camp for girls nearby. That was a little scary but I managed it all right. On Saturday night of my last week, the girls came to Camp Airy for the operetta. When the curtain went up, I swabbed the deck and sang with the other boys, "We sail the ocean blue and our saucy ship's a beauty. We are sober men and true and attentive to our duty...." I still remember the words of all of the songs in the play. It is my favorite Gilbert and Sullivan operetta.

One evening, after a campfire, I slipped away from the other boys and did not go with them to our bunk. Instead, I found a clear space in one of the fields, laid down, and looked up to the sky. For the first time, I saw the heavens as I had never seen them before. I saw the Milky Way. I recognized constellations I had known only from a star map—the Big Dipper, Orion. More stars came into view. I was dazzled. I thought this was because the western sky was different from the sky in Baltimore. I thought about how far away the stars

`

were. I thought about space. I tried to understand how space could end. What was beyond space? What would that be? I tried to figure this out but of course, I couldn't. Finally I decided that I might go crazy if I thought about this too much so I ended my evening of stargazing. I went to bed that night still puzzled about the mystery of space. One thing I did know for sure: going to camp had expanded my universe and I could survive being away from home.

After the first week, it began to dawn on me that we were not out West. I didn't ask anyone because I was afraid I would look foolish for not knowing. By the end of the second week, I was sure we were still in Maryland. I realized that we were only in the western part of the state, not the western part of the country. The hills were the foothills of the Appalachian Mountains. They were not the Rocky Mountains. I was wrong about the geography but right about the adventure. Going to camp was a more

`

exciting journey than anything I could ever
have imagined.

`

27

THE WHITE SWEATER

My older brother, Sidney, home from college, was unfortunately burdened with the responsibility of looking after his younger siblings. Sadly for him, this cocky 13-year old brother did not take kindly to Sidney's role as surrogate parent. Rebellious skirmishes often took place. Finally, on one hot summer evening, the simmering embers of discontent erupted into a full- scale conflagration. A classic drama of epic proportions unfolded.

Usually, after dinner, I could leave the house without notifying anyone, stay out as long as I wished and return home, often with no one noticing. I had grown accustomed to enjoying evenings of benign neglect. But, in truth, at times it felt less than benign, more like neglect. One night, I had decided to hang out with my friend,

`

Itzy Wilder, who lived a block away on Appleton Street. I was confidently striding toward the front door when Sidney stood in my way. He questioned my intention to leave the house without his permission. So, did I feel cared for? No way. He had the nerve to ask me where I was going. "None of your business" didn't go over very well with him. It merely raised the stakes.

Pretty soon, we were locked in a knock-down-drag-out, full-scale battle. "You can't go out. It's too late," he said. That did it. If this was caring, who needed it? I had looked forward to having Sidney at home, but he didn't seem to get it: I expected him to conform to my expectations of him, but I had no intention of conforming to his expectations of me. Now I was trapped. I seethed with rage. How to get back at him? I'll show him! What happened next was not one of my shining moments but, at the time, one of the most gloriously satisfying acts of revenge I could have imagined.

`

Sidney had come home from MIT sporting a brilliant white sweater emblazoned with a letter "M," which he had won for lacrosse. Sidney was very proud of this sweater and he wore it often. Very impressive. I knew exactly where in his room Sidney kept his beloved sweater. After our fight, I made a beeline to his room. I opened the bottom bureau drawer. There it was, pristine and inviting: his MIT sweater, resting comfortably. I lifted the sweater and carefully spread it out on his bed, extending each sleeve. I smoothed it to ensure there were no wrinkles. My next stop was the bathroom.

We kept a bottle of iodine on hand for cuts and scrapes. It was always there in case of an injury. There had certainly been a serious hurt. My pride was bleeding excessively. It was an emergency. Iodine was required. I opened the medicine cabinet, removed the bottle of iodine and returned to Sidney's room. There was the sweater, extended helplessly across his

`

bed, innocent and unprepared for what was to happen next.

I slowly unscrewed the top of the bottle, tilted it, and deliciously dribbled purplish-grey-black iodine across Sidney's white sweater. Jackson Pollock couldn't have done a better job. As I stood admiring my artistic masterpiece, I heard footsteps down the hall. Sidney was coming! I barely managed to scoot past him as he rounded the corner into his room. I was halfway down the hall when I heard the first heart-rending scream. "My sweater, what have you done? I'll kill you!"

I streaked ahead, Sidney in hot pursuit. Desperate, I abandoned my atheism, totally useless at such a time. "Please, God, help me," I implored. Sidney was gaining on me. I was a goner. I prayed even more fervently for divine intervention. Then, truly in the style of ancient Greek drama, a god appeared out of nowhere to rescue me.

`

My brother Sam, older than Sidney, was also at home. He was in his room trying to read when he heard the commotion. Sidney was flying down the hall. Sam came out of his room to see what was going on and...bam! They collided. Sidney was stopped dead in his tracks. I had been saved. I darted into the nearest closet, hoping to become invisible. I will never know what Sam said to Sidney to calm him down. When I sensed that it was safe, I came out of the closet where I had taken refuge. Slowly and gingerly, as if stepping on hot coals, I walked to my room. As I waited anxiously in my room, the most unimaginable thing happened: Sam came into my room, found me crying and actually comforted me, even though I had done something awful.

Had Sidney disregarded Sam's intervention and killed me instead, I believe a court of law would have found him innocent of murder. A jury would have declared the slaying of his younger brother an act of justifiable fratricide. I remained grateful forever that Sam had protected me and that Sidney had spared my life.

Many years later, at an anniversary celebration for Sidney and his wife Jean, I made a complete confession of the whole affair. Although we were to bring no gifts, I thought that a white sweater would not qualify as a gift but rather, a replacement. Still suffering the pangs of guilt and remorse, I had written to MIT to see if I could find a substitute for Sidney's cherished trophy, his white sweater. Sadly, I was informed that these sweaters were no longer available. I did, however, receive a certificate attesting that Sidney had, in fact earned a letter in lacrosse. I could not restore his white sweater but could instead offer him the certificate, which I presented to him. Sidney's acceptance of this inadequate surrogate at long last eased the conscience of a distraught younger brother.

`

We hugged each other. Sidney whispered in my ear, "I don't remember any of this."

28

O HOLY NIGHT

"Congress shall make no laws respecting the establishment of religion..."

It was the First Amendment to the Constitution. It meant you couldn't have just one religion in the country. It meant there was freedom of religion. I learned about that in a class called Civics. The class was in a special public junior high school that everyone called "49," even though its real name was The Robert E. Lee Junior High School. You had to be chosen to go to this school because it was an accelerated school and you finished junior high in two instead of three years.

The school was in downtown Baltimore on Cathedral Street. It was in a really nice neighborhood with other old buildings. You had to take a streetcar and bus to get there from our house. "49" had been a very small private school and was taken over by the city. It was beautiful. There was a private entrance from the street with two staircases that met in the middle. Each floor had only three or four classrooms. The walls were paneled in wood. There was a beautiful wooden staircase that went up from the middle of the first floor to the third floor. The staircase on the first floor was very wide, open, and curved around like part of a big circle. That's where I once stood and sang "O Holy Night" just before the school's Christmas holiday.

The school was decorated for Christmas. There were green wreaths along the banister of the staircase and all around the school. There was a small Christmas tree with decorations in the front hall. My homeroom class was on the first floor. My teacher's name was Nellie Scarborough. She was old. She had long, bony fingers and a skinny neck. Once, while she was writing with chalk on the blackboard, a boy in the

`

class began talking with another student. Miss Scarborough suddenly wheeled around, reached for an eraser, and threw it at him. We couldn't believe what was happening. We were scared and thought it was funny at the same time. We put our hands over our mouths and giggled.

On the last day of school before the holiday, Miss Scarborough took me aside and told me that I had been chosen to sing before the whole school. I was to sing "O Holy Night." I was younger than most of the other boys in the school and I could still sing really high notes when we sang Christmas carols in our music class. I thought that was the reason I was chosen. We didn't have a rehearsal. I knew all the words by heart and I loved singing Christmas carols. Miss Cohen, my music teacher, was to play the piano and I would sing along with her.

When the time got closer for my performance, I started to get nervous.

`

When I left Miss Scarborough's room on the first floor to stand near the staircase, I got more scared. I was more anxious than I usually would feel when I was in a school play or had to recite in class. I didn't know why. Anyway, it was too late. It was like walking in my sleep. I don't remember how I got there but I found myself looking up the staircase where all the children in the school were gathered to hear me sing. Miss Cohen sat down at the piano and played the first part of the carol. Then she played a chord, looked over at me, and nodded her head. I began to sing.

"O Holy Night! The stars are brightly shining, it is the night of our dear Savior's birth." Wait a minute, I thought. What am I doing singing this in front of everybody? Isn't this a song about you know who? It was OK to sing this in class because everybody was singing along with you, but what would happen when I got to the "C" word? Never. I would never sing the word "Christ" when we sang Christmas carols. I

`

would just stay quiet while everybody else sang "Christ" and then I would resume singing. But I couldn't do that now. I was the only one singing.

The music went along. No problem. I was a long way from that part of the carol. "For yonder breaks a new and glorious morn," I continued. "Fall on your knees," I blasted out. All the while I knew what lay ahead and didn't know what I would do. As I sang, I realized what I had done. I was going against a law. It wasn't about the First Amendment so you could have any religion you wanted. There was another kind of law that I had learned without even knowing it. I didn't learn it in class. I didn't learn it in *cheder* (my Jewish after-school class) or in my Reform Sunday School class at the Madison Avenue Temple. I just knew it was a law. A rule: Jewish children didn't sing the word "Christ" when they sang Christmas carols. It was all right to sing carols but you never sang the "C" word. Never. I just knew that.

`

But here I was. Christ was approaching rapidly in the music. "O night divine…" I reached the upper register with my voice high up in the heavens. "The night when…." I don't remember deciding to do this, but somehow since I knew there was no escape, I decided that if I closed my eyes when I sang Christ it wouldn't count. So I did. I closed my eyes and sang, "…when Christ was born."

I escaped. The heavens did not fall. I appeared to be enthralled in the ecstasy of the music. My eyes closed. Safety. I had found a way of completing the carol without violating the unspoken commandment: never say "Christ." Since my eyes were closed, somehow it didn't count. I had discovered the real meaning of freedom of religion.

`

29

THE MUSIC ROOM

The music room was a place where I could be alone and be aware of nothing but music. Most important, it was not at home. It was on the second floor of the Central Enoch Pratt Free Library at the corner of Mulberry and Cathedral Streets in Baltimore. I learned about the music room from my brother Sidney. He told me that the library had a room you could reserve for yourself to listen to any music you wished. Although a little skeptical, one afternoon after leaving my junior high school, I walked to the library. I climbed the central stairway and was directed to the music room on the left.

The librarian was very understanding. I told her I wanted to use the music room. She said it was available. I could use it for an hour. What would you like to hear? I had no idea. Perhaps you could just select an album from the shelves. Thank you. I'll pick out something.

I looked at the stacks of record albums. It was all classical music. I had no idea of what to choose. I scanned past recordings of Bach, Beethoven, Chopin, Debussy, Gershwin, and hundreds of other albums. I asked for the librarian's help. She thought I might like to start with one of the Beethoven symphonies and she picked an album from the shelf. The records had to be handled carefully. Don't get fingerprints on them and use these special needles. They were made of cactus and honed to a fine point. She showed me into the music room.

As soon as I entered the room, the sense of quiet was immediate. The room was softly lit. There were soundproof materials on the ceiling and there were curtains on each of the walls to absorb the sound. The doors were thick and heavy. There were a few

`

comfortable chairs, some lamps, large speakers in the corners of the room, and a table that housed the phonograph equipment. The librarian showed me how to carefully insert the needle and how to operate the turntable. She said, "Enjoy the music," and shut the door. I followed her instructions precisely, placed the first record of the album on the turntable, sat down and listened.

My mother arranged for me to attend children's concerts on Saturday morning at the Lyric Theatre. I remembered hearing pieces thought to be especially interesting for children—*The Sorcerer's Apprentice, The William Tell Overture, The Nutcracker Suite.* I had been aware of symphonic music as background music on the radio. I had never actually listened to a symphony. Now I was hearing Beethoven. The music filled the room and my body resonated with its intensity. *Ta-Ta-Ta Taaaam*. I was transfixed. The other classical music I had heard was fun but this music was different.

`

I was moved by it. The music surrounded me. Nothing else existed. There was only the music. I was alone and with the music at the same time. Nothing could intrude. I felt safe. Time had stopped. After I listened to all of the records in the album, I replaced them and brought the album to the librarian. I reserved the room for the following week.

I worked my way through the stacks of albums with the guidance of the librarian. I returned week after week to the music room. Eventually, when I entered high school, there was little time for me to continue using the music room at the library. But I remembered the music room as a space where time stood still and I could let go of whatever else was happening in my life to give myself over to music. Music became an important part of my life. When I play or listen to music, I create a room where everything else is suspended. There is only the music.

30

MY SISTER'S MUSIC

The sound of the piano was never soft. I woke out of a deep sleep to hear the familiar music, not just drifting up the stairs, rather erupting in a burst of energy that filled the entire house. It was my sister, Rosalie, announcing herself to the world. The music continued as I dressed and moved out of my room to the stairway that led to our living room. When I reached the landing, I stood still; I did not want to interrupt her. Rosalie was at the piano. She played at full speed. It was music that she played over and over again and perhaps was the only piece in her piano repertoire that she mastered completely: "The Rustle of Spring."

I was transfixed. Rosalie was lost in her music. Sometimes, while she was playing an especially romantic part of the music on the piano, she would burst into song. She swayed with passion as her hands crossed over one another and soared up and down the piano keyboard. She almost seemed out of control. But her playing was a welcome antidote to the atmosphere of tension and sounds of angry shouting and confrontation that sometimes hung like a dark cloud throughout our house. I liked to watch Rosalie play and to listen to her.

At other times Rosalie performed another piece of music. Not on the piano. She sang alone, with just her voice. It was in a different key. Not happy. She sang it slowly and with great feeling. It was in a different language. Yiddish. I understood some of the words but not all. She sang with such intensity that it seemed an exaggeration of the song itself. I knew it was about a man who worked in a restaurant. He had very weak hands. He washed dishes. The words sounded as though he were crying, but I wasn't sure. Rosalie exaggerated the pathos of the song and she sounded like an overwrought opera star, squeezing out every last bit of tragedy.

These two different pieces of music were at polar opposites. How could that be? Had I really remembered the song in Yiddish? Did I invent it? I knew when I was older that Rosalie swung between moods of great energy at one extreme and great despair at another. Had I already known that as a child?

I knew Rosalie's song began with words in Yiddish. Something like "*In restoran hob ich gezen an altn man in kitchen shteyen....*" "In a restaurant I saw an old man standing in the kitchen." I found on the Internet the song that Rosalie had sung many years ago. It was called *Der Dishvasher,* "The Dishwasher," and it began exactly as I had remembered it. As I read farther into the song, my heart sank. "*Ikh vash un bet af zikh aleyn dem toyt.*" It meant, "I wash and pray only for my own death." How awful. How sad. I had heard the music but not the

words. Finally, after all these years I knew
what Rosalie had been singing.

Experiencing her own sadness, Rosalie
developed a sensitivity and sympathy for
the pain in the lives of others. Using her
enormous energy, she became a state
senator and brought about improvements
in health care for people who were ill,
especially the mentally ill. I still carry the
memory of Rosalie's music inside of me. If I
pause, I can still hear not only her piano
playing but also her singing. Two different
keys. My sister's music: two different parts
of her.

31

SHE KNEW WHO I WAS

My parents were not in the habit of letting us know what to expect very far in advance. So it was not unusual for my mother to wake me up one summer morning to announce that we were going on a trip. Where to? We're going to visit Aunt Mitzi and Uncle Al Macklin. But don't they live far away? It's only in North Carolina. Hurry up, get dressed, we're leaving right away. I did as I was told, changed from my pajamas to my clothes, went to the bathroom, ate breakfast quickly, and got in the car.

I sat in the front seat next to my father who, of course, was in the driver's seat. In the back seat, my mother sat with my Aunt Katie. Where were my brothers and sisters? I was afraid to ask. I realized as we drove off that I was going somewhere by myself with my parents. I felt a guilty pleasure in being chosen and to this day, I believe that I was the only one in the family to have ever had this experience. I remained quiet; afraid my father would change his mind, turn around, and deposit me at home again. That didn't happen. We drove off in the early morning light and I dozed off.

I woke up hearing my mother and Aunt Katie shouting at each other. That was familiar to me. Whenever they were together, they seemed to get into a fight about something. I couldn't quite make out what it was about this time. Gradually, it became clear. They were in total disagreement about something that didn't seem very important: What was the right way to get in a car? Do you put your *tuchus* (behind) down first on the seat and then bring your legs in, or do you do it the other way around—legs first, tuchus second? They each quoted some authority to one another. No one was convinced. There

`

were no concessions. As always, it ended in a complete draw.

We drove for hours, stopping for gas and for something to eat. The trip seemed to go on forever. By late afternoon, we were nearing our destination. Aunt Mitzi and Uncle Al ran a small grocery store in a suburb of Raleigh. For reasons I could not understand, Aunt Katie thought it would be fun to send me into the store to tell the Macklins that they had family visitors from Baltimore. I realized that they had not told them we were coming, just as I had not been told in advance that we were going to visit them. I couldn't believe that I was to be the messenger, announcing our arrival. I appealed to my mother. She sided with Aunt Katie. My father kept driving.

I felt in a panic. Aunt Mitzi would not recognize me. I wasn't sure she knew me apart from my brothers. I was known as "one of the Silber boys." In spite of the way I often behaved, I was very shy. Despite my

`

protests, Aunt Katie told me just to go in the store and ask for a Coke. She explained that Aunt Mitzi would be surprised to see me and then I would tell her how I got to her store.

My father leaned over and opened the door. Disagreeing with him would have been inconceivable. I got out of the car and moved very slowly, inch by inch, toward the store. I climbed the few steps that led to the screen door, the store entrance. The door squeaked as I pushed it open. Aunt Mitzi was ringing up the cash register and depositing some money a customer had given her. Moving toward her I said, as I was told, "Could I have a Coke?" I wanted to disappear. This was all a terrible mistake.

"Earle! What are you doing here?" Aunt Mitzi shrieked. She leaned over and gave me a great big hug. A cloud lifted. She knew who I was. She knew my name. After that, everything unfolded as planned. My

`

parents and Aunt Katie triumphantly marched into the store. There were more happy hugs and kisses, shouting, explaining, and laughing. I had performed my role as messenger.

Aunt Mitzi was my mother's youngest sister and my favorite aunt. I thought she was my most intelligent relative. She read books and seemed to know what was going on in the world. When I talked with her, I did not feel like a child. I have always felt grateful to her for recognizing me as a separate person in a family filled with so many aunts, uncles, sisters, brothers, and cousins. She knew who I was. She helped me in more ways than she could have imagined when she called out my name and put her arms around me that summer day a long time ago.

32

WHY WORRY TWICE?

A man suddenly smacked a mask over my face. I couldn't breathe. I was afraid I would suffocate. I screamed. I was terrified.

Everything was white. The man was wearing a white suit. I tried to get free. He just held the mask down even harder. Somebody was holding my hands down on the table. The table was white. I screamed some more. They wouldn't stop. He told me to blow away the gas. I couldn't catch my breath. I looked at him and pleaded with my eyes. Everything was white. There was a bright light. Everything was white.

Then I was in a different white room in a white bed. My throat hurt. It felt sore and it hurt to swallow. My mother gave me some ice in a glass and told me to try to swallow.

`

I could move my arms and legs. Nothing was holding me down any longer. My mother was sitting by my side and tried to comfort me. Why did the man try to stop me from breathing?

My mother said I could have some ice cream. She said I could have as much as I wanted. Why did my throat hurt? What happened to me? Little by little, my mother explained. I was in a hospital. It was called Sinai Hospital. I had an operation. They took my tonsils out. Everybody has his tonsils out. It will make you feel better. I didn't feel better. Why didn't you tell me what was going to happen? I didn't want to worry you. Why should you worry twice?

Little by little, I remembered: my mother woke me up very early that morning. Why did you wake me? Just get dressed. We're going somewhere. Where are we going? Get dressed and you'll see. I went to the bathroom. When I came back to my room, my mother had some clothes ready for me.

Get dressed, we have to hurry. I wanted to eat something for breakfast but she said I couldn't have anything. Why wouldn't my mother let me eat?

We went downstairs to the kitchen and then down a few more stairs into the "shipping room." It was a room where everything that came from the bakery was stored on shelves before they were shipped out to the different stores. Dave Gordon was waiting for us. He was in charge of the delivery trucks, and he was going to drive us somewhere this morning.

I got in front between Dave Gordon and my mother. Nobody said anything. We drove up Monroe Street and turned on North Avenue. We went past one of the stores and I asked, why didn't we stop there? You'll see. It was quiet in the truck. We came to a place I hadn't known before and I looked at the street sign: North Broadway. We turned down the street, and

`

finally we came to a huge building surrounded by a lot of other big buildings.

Everything happened very fast. The building smelled funny. It was like the smell in Dr. Kirsh's office. My mother took me to an elevator and we went up to a room. A lady in a white dress said I had to take off my clothes. I turned to my mother. She nodded yes. I did what the lady said but I turned away from her because I didn't want her to see me naked. She gave me a white robe to put on. I had to put it on backwards.

Soon someone came pushing a white table on wheels and they told me to climb on the table. My mother didn't go with me. I lifted myself up to see if she was following but someone pushed me back down on the white bed. They rolled the bed past some big doors into a room with very bright lights.

`

A man suddenly smacked a mask over my face.

33

LAMB CHOPS

Elementary school was only a few blocks away from my house. I walked every day across Westwood Avenue to Appleton Street, turned left and headed south, crossing Presbury and Baker Streets until I arrived at Pressman Street, the location of P.S. 29. The school was a rambling one-story wooden structure, set on a large lot with plenty of space to play. It was truly a neighborhood school, near enough to where we lived that we had ample time to go home for lunch in the middle of the day before returning for the afternoon.

Lunch was not a casual meal. There was little variation in the menu. In spite of also working in the store, helping with shipping bakery goods to the branch stores, and supervising feeding many of the bakers, my mother always managed to have lunch

`

ready on time. She regularly served me lamb chops. They were no ordinary lamb chops. They had plenty of juicy fat that I think my mother felt was essential for a growing boy. Usually there were also potatoes or other vegetables. And, of course, I could choose any dessert I wished from the bakery. Well, not exactly. My choice was limited to any bun, éclair, cookie, pie, or pastry that was mashed, mangled or otherwise unsuited for sale in the store. But what I remembered best were the lamb chops, the centerpiece of the lunch. I had no idea how special these lamb chops were until many years later.

Well into our seventies, my brother Sam and I were given to reminiscing about our childhood. We talked about growing up on Monroe Street. We compared notes. We exchanged recollections about going to elementary school at a time when we came home for lunch each day. Up to a point, our memories were quite similar. But when we compared the menu for lunch, our memories diverged. Quite innocently, I recalled, "Mom gave me lamb chops every day. She never missed." I was totally unprepared for Sam's reaction.

Sam looked incredulous. His jaw dropped. He was shocked. "What? Mom gave you lamb chops?" he exclaimed. "She gave me scrambled eggs and spinach. I can't believe it. You had lamb chops?" he uttered with an air of total disbelief. I had indeed struck a nerve. I tried to soften the blow. "Maybe it wasn't every day," I added. That only seemed to make matters worse. I changed the subject.

Later that evening, the phone rang. My oldest brother Bernard was on the phone, calling from California. We exchanged pleasantries. Then his tone changed. "I was just on the phone with Sam. He told me that you had lamb chops for lunch when you came home from school. Is that true?" he asked. I had to confess. "Yes," I admitted. There was no denying that I had lamb chops. I knew what was coming next. He too, had scrambled eggs with spinach. He couldn't believe it. News of my lamb chops spread like wildfire and there were similar calls from other members of the family. Obviously, I had created quite a sensation in the Silber family. I dreaded answering the phone until the calls from my indignant brothers and sisters finally came to an end. I bore their outrage with great nobility.

I learned that my younger sister, Evelyn, was also the recipient of the same notorious lamb chops. If I had only known as a child that my mother had prepared something for me that she didn't fix for all of my brothers and sisters, I would have savored my lunches all the more. Probably, the bakery had prospered enough by the time I was born that my mother felt she could afford lamb chops for me. In all honesty, my recollection of the lamb chops was that they were very greasy and overcooked. But, that's beside the point.

They were, after all, lamb chops—not scrambled eggs and spinach.

34

TAYGLACH

Tayglach are balls of dough boiled in honey, encased in honey, and stuck together with honey. When you eat them, they are crunchy, almost hard, but easy to bite into. As they melt in your mouth, the sweet, sweet taste of honey dances on every taste bud and is delicious beyond any other candy I have ever eaten. My grandmother, my Bubbe, made tayglach. There was always a small dish of it on a table next to a big easy chair in Bubbe's living room. She made tayglach especially for Rosh Hashanah but I remember them as always being available in her house whenever I visited her.

Bubbe was huge. When she hugged you, it was hard to breathe. Her large arms enveloped you and smothered you into her big, overgrown belly, which hung like an

apron in front of her. She smelled of soap.
Often on my way home from Easterwood
Park, I would stop in to see her. Her house
was on the corner of Ruxton Avenue and
Presbury Street, a few blocks west of
Monroe Street, where we lived. There was
a row of hydrangeas with blue blossoms
that grew on the side of the house. Inside,
in the living room, were the tayglach,
always in the same place, waiting to be
eaten. Bubbe never seemed to object to my
eating as many as I wanted.

When I would become rambunctious,
running when I was asked to stop,
wrestling with my cousin, or misbehaving,
I would be reprimanded by aunts and
uncles who lived with Bubbe. Bubbe would
wave them away and repeat in Yiddish,
"*Luz em gemacht, luz em gemacht,*" which I
learned translated to "Let him be, let him
be." She was my protector. Her
intervention and her tayglach were the
welcome antidotes to the harsh criticism
rife in my family.

`

When I was nine, one morning I was awakened by Mozella with bad news. "Your Bubbe has died," she told me. I was furious. "Don't say that! That's not true!" I yelled at her. I refused to believe it. Mozella had made this up. I could not accept that Bubbe was dead. Mozella was only playing a trick on me. That was very mean. But later that day, I was taken to Bubbe's house. It was different than ever before.

The house was quiet. There were people everywhere. They were talking with soft voices. The mirror in the hall was covered with a cloth. I didn't understand why. From the living room, I caught sight of a coffin on the dining room table. I was afraid to look at it too carefully. I did not want to go any closer. There were candles. A rabbi was mumbling prayers in Hebrew. I looked instead toward the table near the large chair in the living room. There were no tayglach. My Bubbe was dead.

`

I sat silently in the car as we drove to the cemetery. I was numb. I was cold. I had never been inside a cemetery. The car emptied and everyone assembled into a narrow line and followed the casket past the gate that opened into a forest of marble tombstones. I was told I could not go inside; it was forbidden because I was a Kohen. "What's that?" I asked. I was shushed. "Kohens are priests who come from a special tribe. Your father is a Kohen, so you are, too. Kohens are not allowed to go near a dead body, so you can't go inside the cemetery."

I stayed close to the entrance and watched at a distance. Words were murmured I could not make out. The casket was being lowered into the ground. That finally meant to me that Bubbe really was dead. They don't bury people who are still alive.

Suddenly, there was the terrible sound of screaming. My Aunt Katie was hysterical, shouting, flailing her arms, throwing her

`

head back and yelling at the top of her lungs. She was trying to jump into the grave. People held onto her and got her to stop and to quiet down. I was frozen in place. I had never seen anything like that before. I was very frightened. I was bewildered. I saw my mother crying. That made me feel very bad. I finally began to cry.

There is a postscript. When I was living in New York in a small garden apartment with Carol and our newborn son, Stevie, my mother visited. She brought with her a small box of tayglach that she had made for us. I bit into one. It was not exactly like the ones Bubbe had made. They were hard to dent, took more energy to eat, and didn't quite taste the same as my Bubbe's tayglach. But I was delighted to chew on them once again and I thanked my mother profusely for bringing them. That was all my mother needed to hear to stir her into action, making batch after batch of

`

tayglach that she mailed to me at regular intervals after she returned home.

I ate one or two of the tayglach after they arrived, but usually, the time in transit required by the postal service at that time rendered them more like little cannon balls than candy. I tried eating them, but couldn't. I also couldn't throw them out. Time went by and pretty soon the top of the kitchen closet was filled with many of my mother's unopened packages of tayglach. Carol pleaded with me to get rid of them. I could not. Soon, we had the largest collection of tayglach in any Jewish household in the entire New York area, if not the world.

My struggle with wanting to make room in the closet to please Carol and also wanting to hold on to my tayglach was finally resolved when I was called into the Army. We had to pack up, leave New York, and head for Texas. "Surely you're not going to take the tayglach with us?" Carol pleaded. I realized there was no solution but to get rid of them. I couldn't actually perform the deed myself. I asked Carol if she would clean them out when I was out of the kitchen. She did. I was sad. I knew that I had probably eaten my last tayglach. Over time, that didn't matter.

The tayglach were gone. But not the memory of my Bubbe. She continues to comfort me.

35

THE END OF POSSIBILITIES

My brother Myer tormented me. I could never escape. He was four years older and I wanted more than anything for him to be my friend. He teased me instead. I was desperate for his affection, so I never learned to ignore his hurts. Instead, I pleaded with him, tried to fight back, cried, and responded to his meanness by exposing my vulnerability over and over again. He made up silly rhymes about me that he would chant in a mocking way. I couldn't stand hearing them.

When we were at the beach, he knew how to use sand as a weapon and how to destroy carefully constructed castles. Eventually, I gave up my pursuit of winning him over. It wasn't reasoned, but I think I just became exhausted and finally had enough sense to know that the best

`

relationship I could have with Myer would be at a distance.

Myer provoked my father. As a child, I blamed Myer for causing my father to be angry. If Myer would only behave, my father would be nice. It was Myer's fault that my father blew up at him. I hated the scenes. I was terrified when my father struck him, beat him, and especially when he hit Myer in the face. I couldn't really accept how cruel my father was. I made Myer responsible instead. If only Myer were different, we would have peace in the family.

Myer did bad things with girls. I didn't know exactly what they were, but I heard much yelling about that, even from my mother. He must have done really bad things if my mother got angry at him. She rarely raised her voice at me. It was all very simple: I was good; Myer was bad. But I was attracted to his badness and wanted to find out more about it. When Myer was out of the house, I would slip into his room and search his desk. I was richly rewarded.

Myer's desk was a treasure trove of dirty comic books. They were my first manuals about sex. There was Popeye and Olive Oyl doing *it.* Even Dick Tracy and Tess Truehart did *it.* And in every position anyone could imagine. This was really great. Myer was really bad and I could reap the benefits of his badness without anyone being the wiser.

Sometimes there were fights on the street. I was very frightened watching people hitting one another. I pleaded with Myer not to join in. He was a fighter. I cowered. I blamed Myer for causing trouble. His willingness to fight frightened me. Myer did not do well at school. By default, he seemed to be the only one of the family who was going to continue to work in the bakery. But history intervened.

We were at war. Myer enlisted in the Army Air Corps. He was sent off somewhere in the South for training and in a short time, he became a navigator. Everything seemed to move quickly. Myer came home from training and looked very handsome in his Army uniform. He said goodbye to us before he was sent overseas. From his letters, we learned that Myer was now part of a crew flying bombing missions over Germany.

Contrary to my earlier feelings about him, I began to feel a sense of pride in Myer. We never had become friends as I had so desperately wished as a child. Maybe, when the war was over, this would happen. Maybe Myer was really changing. People can change. Myer might come back a different person. Maybe we would get along. Why not? It was a possibility.

But one day, some people from the Red Cross were at the door. I regret to inform you. Oh no. Oh God, no. Over England.

Returning from a mission. Everyone was killed. The plane had been damaged. Was buried in Cheltenham. Please come in. Let us know if there is anything we can do. Possessions will be sent. Yes, over England. Returning from a mission. Everyone was killed.

My father was devastated. His eyes were swollen and red. I had never seen him cry. For the first time, I felt compassion for him. When Myer's trunk came, we went through all of his possessions. I claimed his watch. It was all that I had of Myer. I still own it. It stopped at nine nineteen. That must have been the time of the crash. It reads on the back *Property of US Army AF.*

There were no more possibilities. He would never be transformed as I had wished. I grieved. Not because of my attachment to Myer; that was long gone. I grieved because there would no longer be any connection. He was not going to

`

return, transformed into a brother I wish I had had. This was the end of possibilities.

My father died not long after Myer was killed. Several years later, Myer's body was brought home and there was another burial, this time near my father's grave.

36

UNCLE JAKE SILBER

My father's brother, Jake, manufactured men's clothing. But by far, his greater talent lay in his ability to comment about life with irony and wit. He spoke with a heavy accent and he exemplified Yiddish humor. I was eternally grateful to him for helping me through a moment in my life that otherwise would have been unbearable.

I had been up most of the night. My father was lying on the couch in the living room, breathing with the help of an oxygen mask. Milton Kirsh, the family doctor, had been with him most of the evening, and needed to rest. He asked me to look after my father and went upstairs to bed. I was left alone in the room with my father. It was agonizing. I tried not to sleep but dreaded remaining awake. My father lay dying.

I distracted myself by reviewing the anatomy of the circulatory system in my mind. I traced the path of the aorta as it left the heart and provided blood to every part of the body. I did not want to think about my father's heart and its failure. When his breathing became irregular, I froze in terror. I called for Milton. He came but there was nothing more that could be done. My father did not move. The balloon of oxygen had stopped expanding and contracting and was now motionless and shriveled. My mother was waiting in the kitchen. I told her he had died. It was early morning, before dawn. I went to bed.

When I awoke from a fitful, restless, and exhausting sleep, I came downstairs where Uncle Jake was conferring with my mother. They had decided that I should go with my Uncle to the funeral home to make arrangements. I was the only one of my brothers at home. I suppose my sister Libbye, although older than I, was disqualified because of being female. I would have gladly surrendered the honor to her. I was bleary eyed and drained. I couldn't imagine anything more difficult than taking part in the business of planning my father's funeral.

I got in the car with Uncle Jake. We had little to say to one another. He drove down Liberty Heights Avenue to Garrison Avenue, turned right, and after a few miles, at Walbrook Junction, we headed east on North Avenue. We parked in front of Levinson's Funeral Home. I emerged from the car and felt as if I were walking through heavy syrup. Uncle Jake went ahead. When inside the funeral parlor, as it was euphemistically called, we were greeted by an unctuous salesman.

As Uncle Jake began the process of negotiating the cost of the funeral I studied the tiles in the ceiling. We were ushered into a room filled with row upon row of caskets. I shifted my attention to the design in the rug. I couldn't bear to look or to hear the bargaining.

I tried to distract myself. This could not really be happening. I did not want to hear what was being said. It was no use. The bargaining going on around me continued. "Best quality pine." "Difference in price." "Yes, but what about the liner for the casket?" God, I did not want to listen. I closed my eyes as if that would also close my ears. Nothing helped. My uncle was in the midst of negotiating the remaining details of the funeral. The funeral director was describing everything that would be provided including clothing for my father. A shroud? A suit? I wasn't sure what was being discussed. I struggled not to hear.

Finally I realized that some sort of contract was being prepared. It had boiled down to two different packages, one more expensive than the other. How could my uncle continue to bargain at such a moment? But he did. A price was agreed upon. He hesitated before making a final decision. He looked thoughtful and paused, pen in mid-air, before signing the agreement.

At last he looked at the salesman and, in his thick Yiddish accent, said, "Tell me, Mister Levinson, vid de more hexpensive funeral..." he hesitated, then continued, "Vill my brudder be buried in a suit vid vun or two pair of pants?"

I looked up at my uncle. He smiled at me. I smiled back. We both began to laugh. The cloud evaporated. I would be able to manage this. Thank you, Uncle Jake.

37

DO NOT DISTURB

I have no memories of my father ever praising me. I only associated him with fear. As much as I could, I avoided encounters with him. I could never be sure what would trigger his rage. I was terrified as a child when he flung dishes against the kitchen wall in a storm of fury. His fights with my brothers taught me to try to become invisible to him. The dull thud of his fist beating against my brother Myer's face made me sick. My father died when I was twenty. I believed there was something fundamentally wrong with me because I felt only relief at his death and was incapable of feeling sadness.

Ike Silber's funeral service was at the synagogue, our *shul*. He was much revered because he was, outside of the family, very generous. I have already written that

`

during the Depression he had fed the poor with bread from his bakery that had been left over from the day before. People came to him when they were in need and I often witnessed him giving money to itinerant rabbis who would come to the door.

I sat huddled down on one of the benches in the shul. I listened to the rabbi's eulogy, recounting my father's extraordinary consideration of those in need. He went on, as I somehow knew he would, about how grateful the synagogue was for all that Ike Silber had done to help his neighbors when they were in need. Nothing he said was not true. My father was greatly admired.

It was very hot in the shul. I was in a deep sweat. Perspiration seeped through my woolen suit. I was painfully uncomfortable, not as much from the heat and the bad ventilation in the shul as from my anxiety and confusion. I could not fit together the rabbi's image of my father with the other image of him that was imbedded inside me.

It had been essential in growing up to remember that my father was dangerous. Otherwise, I would be unprepared for the sudden way he could ridicule me just when I believed I could trust him to act kindly.

I listened and felt distant from the rabbi's eulogy. Suddenly, I became very attentive. The rabbi was telling a story about one of Ike Silber's sons. As the story unfolded, I realized it was about me. I was dumbfounded. My father had actually talked to the rabbi about his pride in me. His son had learned to be generous and to share his own good fortune with others in need, just as Ike Silber had. With exalted, flowery speech, the rabbi recounted an incident my father had shared with him:

> One afternoon, as was his habit, Ike took a nap on the living room couch. When he awoke, his son told him that while he was sleeping some rabbis came to the door asking for money. His son, not wanting to awaken his father,

asked the rabbis to wait for a moment. He then went to his room, took some money from his own savings and gave a few dollars to the rabbis. What a *mitzvah*! What a blessing, the rabbi exclaimed. The son had taken on the values of the father. Praise the heavens! A father's true legacy. How proud Ike was of his son.

How proud of his son? Why had he shared his pride with the rabbi but not with me? Why had he died without ever telling me? I was angry. The son in the story was being generous. That was not my recollection. I remembered that day quite well.

When my father napped, he was not to be disturbed. Not for anything. Period. Nothing. My father had already fallen asleep in the living room. I happened to be in the hall when, through the windows of the doorway, I spotted two rabbis, easily identified by their long, black coats, wide-brimmed flat hats, long ringlets of hair, and full beards. They were approaching when I ran quickly to the door and opened it quietly before they could knock or ring the doorbell. If my father had been awakened, I knew he would explode and I would become the target of his boiling rage for disturbing him. The old terror spread through my body. I did not understand the rabbis' Yiddish exactly, but I knew enough to know that they wanted money. I dashed up the stairs, ran quietly to my room, my heart pounding. I found a few dollars, tiptoed gingerly down the stairs, gave the rabbis the money and, with my finger to my lips, indicated they were to leave quietly. Thank God! My father slept through all of this. When he awoke, I told him what had happened. He said nothing.

I felt confused, listening to the rest of the funeral service. Afterwards, I got in one of the cars headed for the cemetery. The funeral procession passed in front of the shul. The doors of the shul were open wide. Why? I asked my uncle. It was a sign of respect for someone greatly honored, he explained. More shame. Why could I not feel proud of my father as a great man? I could not stop thinking about the rabbi's words. How dishonest I felt.

My father's posthumous praise was not deserved. I had not acted out of generosity. That was not what I had felt. I had really acted out of fear. Now, I felt like a fraud. Instead of pleasure in hearing that my father took pride in me, I felt anger for never having heard him express it directly to me. I never told anyone what had really happened that afternoon when my father napped and I stood guard, as always, afraid of his being awakened. When my father slept, there was peace in the house.

I had, after all, once managed to please my father. But now he was dead. He had already died inside of me a long time ago. It no longer mattered.

38

NO SUBSTITUTES

I was in need of a father. My oldest brother, Bernard, was a very eligible candidate. By the time I was six, he had gone away to college and by the time I was ten, he was a medical student at the University of Chicago. I knew him only during his brief visits home on school holidays. I had a very romanticized view of him.

He was intelligent. He knew the ways of the world. He read books. He knew about politics. He knew folk songs. He knew about the labor movement. He knew about science. When he became a doctor, he was the family consultant on all things medical.

On my birthdays, he gave me children's classics such as *Lorna Doone* and *Black Beauty*. On other birthdays, he sent me a chemistry set and once, a globe of star constellations after I wrote him that I was interested in astronomy. Later birthday gifts included books about poverty in the South and about the Spanish Civil War, all part of an education that no one else in the family could provide. I treasured a gift that he sent me on my sixteenth birthday, *The Life of Sir William Osler*, a biography of one of my great heroes of medicine. I do not remember consciously choosing to be like Bernard, but as I look back, it is obvious that he was my model of how to be a grown man, sophisticated in the ways of the world, an American with a social conscience

Without his realizing it, Bernard was responsible for my early interest in becoming a psychoanalyst. As my older siblings went off to college, they brought home books to add to our library. Among this collection, I found a book of Bernard's titled *The Case of Miss R*, by Alfred Adler, an early disciple of Freud's. At age fourteen, I was intrigued by the title and began

`

reading it with fascination. I couldn't put it down. It was a case history replete with intimate sexual details of great interest to a teenager. I had never read about the struggles and conflicts of a person's life described in such an open and candid way. I felt that Dr. Adler also understood me as well as Miss R. I decided then and there that I would become a psychoanalyst.

At that time, the only path to becoming an analyst was through medical school. That suited me. Bernard had already paved the way. My choice of medicine was certainly also influenced by my admiration for Bernard. Looking back, I can see that even my handwriting began to resemble Bernard's, although his style was unique and difficult to emulate since he had become a serious calligrapher.

After my father died, Bernard felt it was his job to manage and control the family. He changed and became a more complex, sophisticated, and accomplished version of my father: autocratic, controlling, demeaning, cruel with those closest to him and, at the same time concerned with broad issues of social justice in the world outside of the family. I stood up to Bernard, challenged him, confronted him, and rebelled against his assumed authority. Bernard and I became a volatile mix when we were together. He was far different from the Bernard I remembered from my childhood.

But I came to recognize that I also contributed to the antagonism between us. I was angry with Bernard because he was not my father. Not only that, but he was not the ideal father that I wished him to be. Once I was clear about that, Bernard simply became my irritating, impossible older brother who had taken good care of me when I was a child. No one, not even he, could be the father I had always wished for. I would always miss that. There are no substitutes.

39

ONE OF THE LAST TO GO

The night before was much like the others but there was one difference. This was the last campfire. The sparks shot up in the air as the fire died out. I looked up to the sky to follow them as they matched the stars and faded away. The fire was hot, but even so I felt a little chilly. We were singing our camp song for the last time. I still remember all of the words:

> *We are the boys from Airy Camp*
> *You hear so much about*
> *The people they all like us*
> *Whenever we go out....*

We didn't so much sing as yell as loud as we could. It was like singing "The Star Spangled Banner," but we cared more about our camp than we did about anything else that night. When the

`

campfire was over, it was time to go up to our bunks. We walked slowly. I didn't want camp to be over.

The next morning was different. After we got up, used the bathroom and got dressed, we didn't make our beds as usual. We folded up the blankets and put the sheets in the pillowcase and gave everything to our counselor. We weren't going to sleep there anymore. We got out our trunks and opened them. I had not worn any of the clothes on the bottom. It was always easier to take what was on the top and leave the rest. I threw all of my dirty clothes on top, pushed them down and locked the trunk. It was ready to go.

Walking up the hill to have breakfast took longer than usual. We joked, pushed each other, laughed, pretended to be drunk, staggered, picked weeds, and zigzagged across the trail to make the hike last longer. We stopped at piss rock to bid it a last farewell. At the Mansion, there was the early morning flag raising, saluting, and boring announcements. We were told what to do about all the arrangements for going home. Finally, we dragged ourselves into the dining room to our tables. Breakfast was great, especially the big plates full of pancakes, piled high on top of one another, soggy and not really hot; but with lots of butter and oceans of syrup flooding them, they were the best I ever remember eating. Their lingering sweet taste was the taste of camp itself.

After breakfast, everything seemed to go very fast. We made our way down the hill, joined with our friends, feeling sad but never saying so, horsing around, telling the same old jokes, pretending to be having as much fun as always. When we got near our bunks, there were cars down the road. Some of the boys' parents were already there, waiting for them. Saying goodbye to friends who were leaving was a blur. We didn't take much time. "See ya," "Take it easy," "Come back next year," "So long,"

`

"Bye"—mostly with a wave of the hand and certainly no hugging.

Some of us were left. There were fewer and fewer campers. Some were going back by train and went in a bus with one of the counselors. There were bunches of boys under a grove of trees near our bunk. It wasn't far from where we had our last campfire. I could still smell the ashes and remember the night and especially the brightness of the stars in the sky. It seemed like a long time ago, even though it was only the night before. A few boys were left. The numbers grew smaller and smaller. One by one, they peeled away. Cars came and went. Each time, one more friend said goodbye.

Now there were only one or two boys with me. I waited. I saw the car driving slowly up the road and recognized it. It was our car. My parents had come to bring me home. My eyes had water in them. I was brave. I didn't want anybody to see. I didn't want to go home. I loved camp. The two weeks I spent there were the happiest time in my life. I didn't want it to be over. I wanted to stay. I knew you couldn't stay forever.

The car came to a stop near where I was waiting. My mother and father got out. I hugged my mother. We attached my trunk to the back of the car. I got in the back seat. They asked how it was. How could I tell them what it was really like? I settled for, "It was good." My father started the car. I turned and looked out of the back window. My eyes were blurry. I couldn't see clearly. I wanted to hold on. We drove away. Everything got smaller and smaller. I could barely see some of the boys who were still waiting to be picked up. I was one of the last to go.

BIOGRAPHY

Earle Silber attended public elementary and high schools in Baltimore; Johns Hopkins and Harvard Universities; and was a graduate of the University of Maryland School of Medicine. He interned at the Michael Reese Hospital in Chicago. After completing his training in psychiatry at Bellevue Hospital in New York, he served in the Army for two years.

He then moved to Washington to work at the National Institute of Mental Health and to train in the Washington Psychoanalytic Institute, where he later became a Training Analyst. He was a Clinical Professor at Georgetown University Medical School, Guest Professor at Ulm University in Germany, and consultant to the National Institute of Mental Health, the Walter Reed Army Medical Center, and the National Naval Medical Center. He was a member of the Group for the Advancement of Psychiatry. He received an award for Excellence in Teaching by the American

Psychoanalytic Association and is a Distinguished Life Fellow of the American Psychiatric Association. He retired from a career in teaching and the private practice of psychiatry and psychoanalysis in 2005.

He was married to Carol Mayerberg, with whom he had three children: Steve, Rick, and Larry. After Carol's death, he married Judith Jaffe Tolmach and is the stepfather of Jessica and Matt. He now lives with his wife in Chevy Chase, Maryland, where he keeps up with his nine grandchildren, writes, plays the flute in various chamber music groups, continues to play tennis, and occasionally decorates birthday cakes for some of his family and friends.

`

Miniver Press is a publisher of non-fiction ebooks and print books, specializing in history and culture. See more about us at http://www.miniverpress.com or contact us at editor@miniverpress.com

Made in United States
North Haven, CT
08 December 2021

12130138R00141